HERBS
FOR COOKING AND HEALTH

D0543265

Text by
Christine Grey-Wilson

Illustrated by
Jill Coombs

COLLINS
LONDON AND GLASGOW

First published 1987
© Copyright in the text Christine Grey-Wilson 1987
© Copyright in the illustrations Jill Coombs 1987

ISBN 0 00 458826 6

Additional illustrations by Mark Fothergill (pages 58-9, 80-1, 112-13,
204-5, 216-17, 222-3), Christine Grey-Wilson (pages 7-37) and
Elizabeth Rice (pages 52-3, 114-15, 136-7, 170-3)

Colour reproduction by Adroit Photo Litho. Ltd, Birmingham
Filmset by Wordsmiths, London
Printed and bound by Wm Collins Sons and Co Ltd, Glasgow

Reprint 10 9 8 7 6 5 4 3 2 1 0

Contents

About this book

This book covers an interesting selection of everyday herbs, some familiar, many less so. The information, especially medicinal and historical data, is mainly derived from European herbals. The herbs are all easily grown in temperate climates and many can be found wild in parts of Europe.

The plants are to be found in their flowering families, for which both English and Latin names are given in the contents list. The families are arranged alphabetically according to their latin names, so we start with the Periwinkle Family (Apocynaceae) and end with the Violet Family (Violaceae). For those familiar with the families this gives a short cut to finding the plants. Within each family plants are, as far as space permits, arranged alphabetically by scientific names, but English common names are also used throughout. Abbreviations of latin names are used when they are repeated on a page, so *Mentha piperita* (Peppermint), for example, could be referred to as *M. piperita*.

There are sections on growing and preserving herbs, with ideas on home-made herbal products, and quick-check tables of the herbs which will be easiest to grow and most appealing in your kitchen.

You will find simple herbal recipes for everyday minor ills, but for more complicated extracts and preparations you must ask your herbalist.

Introduction

We have been using and enjoying herbs for centuries, using them for flavouring, preserving, colouring, for medicines, perfumes, fly repellants and cosmetics – the list is endless. This book contains a selection of useful, easily-grown herbs, suitable for any garden. Whether you have a traditional walled garden, a small patio or even a windowbox there is always room for a few herbs.

From the earliest times man gathered herbs from the wild for cooking and medicines and many traditions and superstitions built up around them – especially those used as medicinal herbs, which were generally thought to be magical. These traditions were refined and passed on through the years until in the middle ages a sophisticated system of monastery herb and 'physicke' gardens were providing herbal remedies for the populace.

Large houses also had their herb gardens, often with the planting arranged in complicated patterns with attractive walks in between, lined with sweet-scented plants. Even the humblest dwelling would have had its patch of pot-herbs to make a meagre diet more appetising.

With the development of printing, in the fifteenth century, many magnificent books, 'Herbals', were produced. These had simple illustrations and botanical descriptions of plants along with information

about where they were to be found. They also included recipes for various potions which could be prepared from fresh and dried herbs. Nicholas Culpepper's *The Complete Herbal*, produced in English in 1649 and still going today, also included astrological information on each plant. Such details are considered to be less important nowadays.

The plants described by the early herbalists often have vernacular names which give a clue to their properties: for example Self-Heal, Woundwort, Heartsease. Their Latin names do likewise: in *Salvia officinalis* (Sage) the second word – the specific name – *officinalis* would indicate that it was sold by apothecaries; *culinaris* that it was used for cooking; *odorata* or *fragrans* that it had a sweet fragrance.

In the past, when medical diagnoses were less precise than now, many diseases and chronic conditions were attributed to evil spells and witch-craft. Some herbs were thought to be particularly effective against evil. Basil was considered a very powerful antidote to 'bad humours', Angelica root was taken as a 'physicke' to ward off the evils which brought on the plague.

Lightning strikes were thought to be caused by a malevolent 'fluence'. Bay or Holly trees were planted near houses to deflect it. Strong smelling herbs were also considered to be highly potent, especially Garlic, which has always been hugely successful in our house - we have never been troubled by vampires! Recently a farmer swore that he protected his cattle from a foot-and-mouth epidemic by hanging bunches of onions in the cowshed.

Many herbs were also considered, with little proof, to be aphrodisiacs. Nettle seed oil and extracts of Woodruff or Valerian were commonly prescribed for impotence.

In our increasingly technological 'space age' society there is a renewed interest in more 'natural' products – whether they be a bunch of Horsetails to polish furniture, a glass of Chamomile tea to calm the digestion and help sleep or a bunch of Southernwood to repel clothes moths. Herbs are also becoming more popular in cosmetics and perfumes, being less likely to produce allergic reactions than their man-made counterparts.

The domestic remedies in this book should be quite helpful in alleviating minor ailments such as indigestion, sore throats and mild headaches. More serious or persistent ailments should always be taken to your physician, or herbalist. Some herbal medicines require skilled preparation by professional druggists and the methods for making them are therefore not given here, although their usage may be mentioned.

Do not be tempted to experiment wildly with plants. If, for example, an infusion of the leaves of a particular species is recommended, an extract of the fruits or roots should not be taken instead. It may have quite different effects or could even be poisonous. Rhubarb leaf stalks, for example, are delicious, but the leaves are extremely poisonous and make a potent herbal insecticide (see page 168). When you have accurately identified a plant use it only in the ways recommended.

Herb gardens require a minimum of maintenance, once established, and with careful planning, they should provide a continuous supply of interesting and tasty herbs for the kitchen as well as for pot pourri, herb pillows, herbal shampoo and flavourings for drinks. Herbs can supply the vitamins and minerals so often missing from the modern diet and make our food so much more appetising. They really are indispensable.

The herbs in this book can all be readily grown in a temperate climate, or be found in the wild, in Europe. However, it is now illegal to dig up wild plants in Britain and in many other countries. Unless you are absolutely sure of identity *do not* collect any herb from the wild. This is especially true of the umbelliferous herbs, some of which are very difficult to distinguish from related species which are extremely poisonous.

Our wild plants are disappearing rapidly, please pick only small quantities. Besides, most are already in cultivation. Most nurseries and garden centres sell wild flower seeds, so grow your own whenever possible, along with the familiar kitchen herbs.

Growing herbs

Instructions for growing individual herbs can be found in the main text. Generally speaking, herbs are easier to grow than other garden plants and less susceptible to common diseases, except mint rust. There is increasing evidence that growing aromatic herbs amongst your vegetables and under fruit trees will discourage some insect pests.

It is worthwhile collecting seeds from the wild to grow at home. The easiest way to sow them is outside, in spring, in a finely raked, moist soil. A plastic tunnel or cloche will protect them from bad weather and give them a good start. Seeds sown indoors in pots or boxes will come up earlier but will have to be acclimatized to outdoor conditions before they can be permanently planted outside. If your herb garden is a windowbox, or pots on a balcony, start the seeds in the same way.

Plants for growing indoors must always have plenty of light and moisture but must not get too hot. Frequent picking will stop them getting too straggly. Indoor herbs are best grown in clay pots, as these allow for evaporation of excess water so that the roots do not become waterlogged. The pots, whether clay or plastic, should stand on a layer of gravel in a tray to allow for drainage and increase the moisture around the plants.

Large tough wooden boxes or barrels are ideal for patios and balconies. Before filling them with soil place a cylinder of wire netting down the centre of the tub, and always water plants down the centre. This will ensure even watering. Do not paint wood preserver inside the tub as this may upset the plants. Before planting up, scrub the tub thoroughly or light some papers inside it to sterilize the surface.

Hanging baskets look very attractive filled with nasturtiums and other trailing plants. Sphagnum moss is the best material for lining the basket, it retains moisture and keeps the soil sweet, but a plastic sheet punched with holes will serve.

The bottom of any container should be lined with broken crocks, to improve drainage, mixed with charcoal to keep the soil sweet. It is best to fill containers with proprietary potting compost, which is sterilized and free from weeds and pests. Herbs should be given a dose of fertilizer or well-rotted compost each spring.

Some essential herbs for small gardens

Most gardeners have only a limited amount of space which could be assigned to herb growing. although, in general, herbs are not as showy as some of our favourite garden plants, a well-tended patch of herbs, or a tub or windowbox, can be most attractive. The tables that follow give a selection of particularly useful herbs.

HERB	GROWTH AND PROPAGATION
Basil	Annual. Sow in May.
Bay	Evergreen. Take cuttings in autumn.
Borage	Annual. Sow in spring.
Caraway	Biennial. Sow autumn or spring.
Chamomile	Annual or perennial
Chervil	Biennial. Sow autumn or spring, in succession.
Chives	Perennial. Sow in spring.

The tables are only intended as a quick guide. For more detailed information on each herb reference should be made to the main text.

Herbs which are generally collected from the wild, even such important ones as Elderflowers, and very large herbs, such as Lovage, have been omitted from the tables.

KEY: D = dries well   F = freezes well

HARVESTING	WHAT TO USE AND USES
Summer. D.	Leaves, with all tomato dishes.
All year. D.	Leaves, for flavouring soups and stews.
Summer. F.	Young leaves and flowers in drinks.
Summer. D.	Seeds, for flavouring cakes and curry.
Summer. D.	Flowers, in tea and pot pourri.
Before flowering. D.	Leaves, dried for 'fines herbes' or fresh in salads.
All summer. D.	Leaves, as garnish.

HERB	GROWTH AND PROPAGATION
Clove Pink	Perennial. Cuttings, or seeds sown in spring.
Dandelion	Perennial. Sow spring.
Dill	Annual. Sow April-June.
Fennel	Perennial. Sow spring.
Feverfew	Perennial. Sow, division or cuttings, spring.
Garlic	Perennial. Plant October or March.
Hyssop	Evergreen.
Lavender	Perennial. Cuttings in spring and autumn.
Lemon Balm	Perennial. Sow spring or divide spring or autumn.
Lemon Verbena	Perennial. Sow spring or divide spring or autumn.

HARVESTING	WHAT TO USE AND USES
All summer. D	Petal tips, in puddings, drinks or pot pourri.
All summer	Young leaves in salads. Roots roasted for 'coffee'.
Before seeds drop. D.	Leaves and tops as flavouring for pickles.
Summer and autumn. D.	Leaves, seeds or roots as flavouring.
All summer.	Leaves, anti-migraine infusion.
When leaves die.	Bulbs, for flavouring.
Just before flowering. D.	Flowers and tops in teas, sausages and puddings.
Summer. D.	Flowers for pot pourri.
Summer. D.	Leaves for tea.
Summer. D.	Leaves for tea.

HERB	GROWTH AND PROPAGATION
Marigold	Annual. Sow spring.
Marjoram (sweet)	As annual. Sow spring.
Marjoram (pot)	Perennial. Sow spring.
Mint (Spearmint)	Perennial. Divide spring and autumn.
Mint (Peppermint)	Perennial. Divide spring and autumn.
Mint (Bowles)	Perennial. Divide spring and autumn.
Mint (Apple and Pineapple)	Perennial. Divide spring and autumn.
Nasturtium	Annual. Sow spring.
Welsh Onion	Perennial. Sow or divide spring or autumn.
Parsley	Biennial. Sow in succession spring and early summer.
Rose Geranium	Perennial, not hardy. Cuttings in autumn.

HARVESTING	WHAT TO USE AND USES
Summer. D.	Petals for salads and colouring rice.
Summer. D.	Leaves and flowers for flavouring.
Summer. D.	Leaves and flowers for flavouring.
All summer. D.	Leaves for tea.
All summer. D.	Leaves for tea.
All summer. D.	Leaves for sauce.
All summer. D.	Leaves for tea and garnishes.
All summer.	Leaves, flowers and seeds for salads.
All year.	Green leaves for salads.
All summer. D F.	Leaves as garnish and flavouring.
All summer. D.	Flowers for flavouring. Leaves for pot pourri.

HERB	GROWTH AND PROPAGATION
Rosemary	Evergreen. Cuttings in spring.
Sage	Perennial. Sow or cuttings spring.
Savory (Summer)	Annual. Sow spring.
Savory (Winter)	Perennial. Sow or divide autumn.
Sorrel	Perennial. Sow or divide spring.
Southernwood	Perennial. Cuttings spring or autumn.
Sweet Cicely	Perennial. Sow or divide spring or autumn.
Tarragon (French)	Perennial. Divide spring and autumn.
Tarrago (Russian)	Perennial. Divide spring and autumn.
Thyme (Garden)	Evergreen. Sow or divide spring.
Violets	Perennial. Root division.

HARVESTING	WHAT TO USE AND USES
All year. D.	Leaves for tea and flavouring.
All summer.	Leaves for tea or flavouring.
Late summer.	Whole herb for flavouring.
Before flowering.	Leaves for flavouring.
Early summer.	Young leaves in soups and salads.
Early summer.	Leaves as insect repellant.
All summer.	Leaves and fruits for flavouring puddings.
All summer.	Leaves as mild flavouring.
All summer.	Leaves as stronger flavouring.
All summer.	Leaves and flowers for flavouring.
Spring.	Flowers for flavouring and pot pourri.

Collecting and preserving herbs

Herbs such as chives, parsley and chervil, which are used fresh, can be picked as required whenever there are enough sizeable leaves. When herbs for garnishing and salads are grown in pots or windowboxes they can be started earlier in the year and moved to sheltered positions in autumn, thus greatly extending the season for fresh herbs. Not all herbs are suitable for this treatment, but most of them can be stored by drying, General instructions for drying are given here, more specialized methods are mentioned in the main text of the book where appropriate.

Herbs for drying can usually be collected two or three times a year. The best flavoured herbs, with a high volatile oil content, are usually picked just before flowering. The oil content is highest in early

morning, when the dew has lifted, before the sun gets too warm. Herbs should be cut off cleanly and handled as little as possible to prevent bruising. A shallow box or basket is ideal to collect them in, so that they are not crushed. Do not gather more than you can dry easily at one time. Herbs quickly lose flavour when they wilt.

Leafy herbs, such as Rosemary, Sage and Bay, can be tied into loose bunches and hung in a shady airy place to dry: an airing cupboard or unsteamy kitchen will do. Herbs should not be hung anywhere dusty. Muddy, dirty or damaged leaves should be discarded, small amounts of dust can be washed off herbs before drying by dunking them in clean water, giving a quick shake and hanging up to dry.

Small quantities of herbs can be dried by hanging them up in paper or muslin bags. In damp weather the drying can be finished off by spreading the herbs on a tray in a cool oven for ten minutes. Once thoroughly dried the herbs must be stored in sealed jars or containers to preserve the volatile oil content. Bouquet garni can conveniently be prepared at this point, the herbs mixed to your own recipe and tied into tiny muslin packets, then stored in sealed containers.

Flowers collected for pot pourri, such as Meadowsweet, Rose petals or the Violets, Geraniums and Marigolds collected for garnishes and puddings, should be gathered in the mornings like leafy herbs and must be handled very carefully. The flowers must be freshly-opened and undamaged and are best dried on muslin-covered screens as shown. The seeds of umbels soon drop when they ripen. Seedheads of Dill, Carraway, Anise, Fennel etc. should be cut just as they are turning brownish, and hung over a piece of clean paper, or otherwise loosely tied into paper bags to collect the seeds. Poppy heads can be treated in the same way.

Roots such as Dandelion, Parsley and Parsnip are usually gathered in autumn, cleaned and stored in a frost-free place for winter use.

Most culinary herbs can be frozen: just pack fresh, clean herbs in polythene bags and freeze immediately. Be sure to label them. Herb mixtures can be frozen together to make it easier to add them to your favourite soups and stews. When unfrozen the herbs will appear rather limp, but will taste excellent. Single Borage flowers or Violets can be frozen into ice cubes for summer drinks.

25

Pot pourri

In the days when standards of sanitation and general cleanliness were not what they are now, houses, churches and public buildings had sweet-smelling herbs, including Mints, Sweet briar, Lavender, Thyme, Hyssop, Tansy, Sweet flag, Balm and Sage, strewn about on their floors to freshen the air. People carried pomanders and nosegays to combat everyday evil smells and believed that they warded off infections and plague. Nowadays sweet-smelling herbs are less necessary, but it is enjoyable to prepare pot pourri and herb cushions to scent our linen and clothes and to deter moths. Every garden must contain a few suitable plants, such as Roses, Sweet peas, Carnations, Lavender, Sage and many more can be easily obtained or gathered from the wild. Large stores often have a counter selling dried lavender, rose petals and mixtures of herbs, but it is more rewarding to grow your own.

Pot pourri and herb bags can be made from almost any sweet-smelling herbs and it is interesting to experiment with your own mixtures. It is best to stick to the same general recipe.

Easy recipe for pot pourri

1 Combine 1.5 litres (3 pints) of dried flowers or leaves of the main perfume with

2 50cc (15fl oz) of other dried herbs to give an interesting mixture. Clove, Allspice, Ginger and dried Orange or Lemon peel can also be added to give a more exotic tang. A few drops of Essential Oils such as Sandalwood, Patchouli, Poppy or Frangipani can also be added, but these make the whole process more expensive. Add one drop at a time until you have the desired effect, too much and the smell will overpower the more subtle scents.

3 As a fixative, add 40g (1½oz) of Orris root (the ground root of *Iris florentina*), 80g (3 oz) of Calamus powder (the ground root of Sweet flag *Acoruis calamus*) or Gum Benzoin, which comes from a tropical tree. These can be obtained from chemists or herbal shops.

4 Preservative must be included to prevent the mixture of herbs from being attacked by insects or mould. Sea salt is cheap and 25g (½ pint) salt crystals should be added to the above mixture. It must be completely dry and can be dried overnight in a low oven. Moisture absorbing silica gel bags, obtained from chemists, should always be secreted in the bottom of a pot pourri container and dried out in the oven now and then. Borax can be used instead of salt.

Flowers and herbs can be collected for pot pourri at any time of the year. Flowers should be gathered in the morning when the dew has lifted and the flowers have just opened, this ensures the maximum volatile oil content. Leaves should usually be collected just before a plant flowers. They should be spread out on trays, or ideally on muslin screens, in a warm, dark, well-ventilated place until crisp and dry.

The airing cupboard is an ideal place for drying herbs, with the door ajar to increase ventilation. Small flowers should be stripped off their stalks and flowers such as Roses and Carnations should have the petals pulled off and dried separately. Larger herbs such as Sage, Mint, Lavender and Tansy can be hung in bunches in an airy, dark place.

When the flowers and herbs are quite dry they should be sealed into airtight jars with some Orris root or other fixative as in the recipe, and can be left until you have dried all your ingredients and are ready to blend the final mixture. Large sweet jars or storage jars are ideal for this and all the ingredients, including a silica bag, should be thoroughly mixed.

This is the point at which you can experiment with your own combination of flowers, herbs Essential Oils, spices and citrus peel. Start off with simple mixtures and spend some time sniffing around before deciding which to mix together, it is not easy to

separate them afterwards if you change your mind! The jars should then be sealed and left in a cool dark place for about six weeks to mature. The mixture can then be put into bags, pots and containers for use.

A more complicated method, which preserves more of the volatile oils, is to half-dry the petals and then to pack them into a jar in layers 13mm (½in) deep with a little salt over each layer. Each layer should be well compressed and new layers can be added every few days after thoroughly mixing the accumulating contents of the jar. The jar can then be left in a dark, cool place for two weeks, by which time the flowers will have formed a block which can be broken into pieces and mixed into a large jar with other ingredients as before. The flowers prepared by this method do not keep their shape or colour but are ideal for cushions and lidded pots and have a stronger scent.

Herb sachets and bags

Small cotton bags tied with ribbons or made in patchwork can be very attractive and when filled with herbs they will scent clothing and linen and keep stored garments smelling fresh. Lavender is the most usual filling but try also Orris root, Meadowsweet, Lemon balm, Thyme, Bergamot, Geraniums, Southernwood and Artemisia or your favourite pot pourri mixture.

Herb pillows

A large herb bag can be tucked under an invalid's pillow and stuffed with Mints, Thyme or Lemon

balm can ease cold symptoms. Many plants help to induce sleep: hops are well known for this, giving off a volatile oil which is soporific and sedative. Try also Chamomile, Thyme, Mints, Rosemary, Lemon verbena, Lemon balm, Lavender and scented Geraniums.

Moth bags

To deter moths fill a bag with equal proportions of Orris root and some Rosemary, Southernwood, Thyme, Mint, Lavender, Wormwood or Tansy, mixed to your liking. This has a less powerful smell than mothballs.

Pomanders

The name pomander derives from the French *Pomme d'Ambre*, or Ambergris Apple, a ball of ambergris (very expensive fixative obtained from whales) mixed with a pot pourri mixture which kept its scent for a long time.

Pomanders can be easily and more cheaply made by mixing pot pourri with beeswax or gum tragacanth. Tragacanth is a vegetable gum, usually bought as a powder which must be made into a stiff consistency with water before mixing in the herbs. It can be rolled into balls and left in a warm place to dry. Beeswax is less expensive. It can easily be melted down, mixed with pot pourri and moulded into balls. It also gives a spicy perfume to the pomander. Beeswax herb candles will give subtle lighting and scent the room at the same time. Pomanders made from porcelain and filled with pot pourri soon lose their scent, the filling could then be replaced by a beeswax ball which retains the scent longer. The finished pomanders can be hung on ribbons inside wardrobes and linen cupboards and placed in drawers. Nowadays pomanders are often oranges stuck with cloves, very sweet-smelling and easy to prepare.

Pomanders, herb pillows and bags of all types make excellent gifts and can be made quite cheaply.

Scented candles

You can make candles with your own favourite fragrance, such as Lavender, Rosemary or Rose petals, from beeswax or paraffin wax, which is easily bought from craft shops.

Beeswax gives a rich honey scent to candles but is expensive – small amounts can be mixed with paraffin wax to good effect. Dried herbs are added to the melted wax before pouring it into moulds. Lavender stalks and Rosemary leaves may have to be cut up with scissors before mixing with the wax, other herbs can be rubbed into small pieces. Try making candles with different varieties of Thyme, Mint, Scented geraniums, Hyssop or experiment with your favourite herbs.

Candles can be coloured by mixing pieces of wax crayon into the melted mixture and powdered or solid dyes can also be obtained from craft shops.

Old tins, glasses and cartons can be used as moulds or you can make your own from thin card. Moulds and wicks can be bought from craft shops. Candle wicks are sold in different sizes, for using with candles of different diameters, or cotton string soaked in boracic acid (obtainable from chemists) can be

used. Always ensure that the wick is firmly anchored to the bottom of the mould before pouring in the melted wax. The other end is tied round a pencil to keep the wick taut. The candle should shrink as it cools and come out of the mould quite easily.

Incense

Dried lavender stalks can be used as joss sticks after removing the flowers. When you are collecting the leaves of Rosemary, Artemesias, Thyme and other herbs do not discarded the stalks. Dry them out and toast a few on the fire to scent the room. Bay leaves, lavender flowers, rose petals and the seeds of Cumin, Angelica, Carraway and many other herbs will also give off a wonderfully warm scent if heated until they begin to smoke.

Scented furniture polish

Sweet-smelling furniture polish can be made from beeswax and real turpentine (not white spirit or turpentine substitute). A few drops of Essential Oils, powdered dried herbs such as Rosemary, Lavender or Rose petals, or even powdered Cinannamon and other spices, can be added to give an exotic aroma to your home.

To make the polish: Over pans of hot water warm separately 275g (½lb) beeswax and 1 litre (1¼ pints) of real turpentine.

WARNING: turpentine is volatile and highly flammable – do not expose it to direct heat or naked flames. Mix the powdered herbs or spices into the melted wax and add this, a little at a time, to the warm turpentine, whisking vigorously. The resulting cream can be stored in wide-topped tins and jars and used to clean the furniture for special occasions. Beeswax and real turpentine are not cheap: a more economical polish can be made by replacing half the beeswax with paraffin wax, but it does not smell as good.

Bath herbs

What better after a hard day's work than to relax into a fragrant bath. A strong decoction of your favourite herbs can be strained off and mixed into the bath water to good effect, but bath bags are easier to use, if less strong. To make bath bags tie dry herbs into cotton or muslin bags and hang them under the hot tap. Even more fragrance is released if they are rubbed on to the body. The bags can be dried out and reused until they lose their scent. Good bath herbs include Chamomile, Mugwort, Feverfew, Lemon verbena, Lemon balm, Lemon thyme, Lavender, Rosemary, Mint, Anise, Fennel and rose petals. Bran or oatmeal added to the bag will help to cleanse the skin but makes the bag more difficult to dry.

Add a delightful freshness to your washing by adding a few drops of Essential Oils or a herbal decoction to the final rinse. Sprinkle lavender water or Rose water on to airing clothes before storing them away.

Herbs for Health

Medicinal recipes

It is important always to use fresh, clean ingredients and equipment when making herbal preparations and, when made, not to store them for to long. Most teas and decoctions will only keep for a day or two and are best prepared fresh as required. Syrups and extracts last longer but are complicated to prepare and are best obtained from a herbalist.

Tisanes, infusions and decoctions, unless otherwise stated, should be taken in a standard dose of 1 wineglass (100cc)three times a day. These are the usual methods of preparing them:

Tisane or infusion: Make in the same way as tea. Pour 60cc (1pint) boiling water over 15g (½oz) dried or 25g (1oz) fresh herb, cover and leave to infuse for at least 10 minutes before straining. (1 tablespoon = about 5g herbal tea mix.)

Decoction: Use the same quantities of herb and water as for a tisane. Bring slowly to the boil in a covered pan and simmer for 5 minutes or so, according to the herb used. Do *not* use an aluminium pan.

Poultices: are usually made from freshly crushed, undried plants and applied, hot or cold as required, to the afflicted part with lint and sticking plaster. They must be made fresh for each application.

Compresses: will reduce swelling, of a sprained ankle for instance. A cold compress of crushed herbs can be bound tightly around the injury with a length of bandage, or a scarf if you are out on a walk.

For more complicated herbal recipes consult specialist publications.

Herbs for common ailments

The following list will give an idea of the huge variety of herbal remedies which can effectively combat everyday ills.

When used in the recommended doses herbs will not be harmful, but do not think that increasing the strength of herbal medicines necessarily produces faster or more lasting results. The opposite may be true. It is always best to stick to the recipes and dosages which have been shown to work by years of practice.

WARNING: What may seem to be a minor complaint could be the symptom of a more serious disease. If symptoms persist always see your doctor or herbalist.

Acid indigestion
Meadow sweet – drink an infusion of flowers and leaves
Mint – drink an infusion of leaves
Acne
Burdock – drink an infusion of herb
Arthritis
Dandelion – drink an infusion
Agrimony – drink an infusion regularly
Nettle – drink an infusion of herb
Asthma
Meadowsweet – drink an infusion of flowers
Backache
Butterbur – drink a decoction
Hawthorn – leaves added to tea
Bad breath
Parsley – chew leaves
Carraway – chew seeds
Bath herbs
Chamomile – see page 35
Valerian – see page 35
Boils
Chickweed – leaf poultice of fresh plant
Broken bones
Comfrey – crushed roots applied as plaster
Burns
Nettles – ask your herbalist
Bruises
Lady's mantle – drink an infusion
Marigold – wash with infusion
Comfrey – drink decoction or infusion

Bronchitis
Coltsfoot – make into syrup
Chestiness
Marshmallow – drink infusion or decoction of root
Horehound – make into candy
Horsetail – drink infusion or spoonfuls of juice
Colds
Yarrow – drink infusion
Horehound – make into candy
Confinement (following)
Lady's mantle – drink infusion
Conjunctivitis
Eyebright – use professional preparations
Constipation
Plantain – seeds made into jelly with water
Coughs
Coltsfoot – made into syrup
Comfrey – drink infusion of leaves and flowers, or
    fresh juice
Mullein – drink infusion
Horehound – make into candy
Dandruff
Burdock – drink infusion
Chamomile – apply infusion to scalp
Diabetes
Sweet Cecily – add to food in place of sugar
Diarrhoea
Blackberry – drink decoction of root or leaves
Meadowsweet – drink infusion of leaves
Disinfectant
Sphagnum – sterile wound dressing

Disinfectant (contd)

Onions – juice is mildly effective

Eyestrain

Always use professional preparations on the eyes –
Rue, Comfrey, Eyebright, Chickweed, Agrimony
and Horsetail are all used by herbalists.

Flatulence

Mints – drink infusion

Chamomile – drink infusion

Fennel – chew a few seeds

Headaches

Feverfew – a leaf or two every day

Chamomile – drink infusion

Hiccoughs

Mint – drink infusion or chew leaves

Indigestion

Chamomile – drink infusion

Mint – drink infusion

Insect repellant

Rue – hang bunches of herbs in room or store clothes
with moth bags

Yarrow – use in bunches or in moth bags

Southernwood – use in bunches or in moth bags

Insomnia

Chamomile – drink infusion

Hops – dried hops in pillow

Intestinal tonic

Marshmallow – drink infusion

Plantains – make seeds into jelly with water

Meadowsweet – drink infusion of leaves

Lumbago
Rue – rub it on

Nausea
Lemon verbena – drink infusion
Mint – drink infusion

Nosebleed
Yarrow – a few leaves up the nose

Nettle sting
Dock – rub leaves on to rash

Rheumatism
Dandelion – drink an infusion of leaves
Horsetail – drink an infusion of leaves
Agrimony – drink an infusion of leaves
Burdock – drink an infusion of leaves
Chickweed – drink an infusion of leaves
Rue – drink an infusion of leaves
Comfrey – drink an infusion of leaves
Meadowsweet – drink an infusion of flowers

Spots
Cleavers – crushed herb as poultice
Burdock – drink an infusion
Elder – wash face frequently in infusion
Periwinkle – ask herbalist for ointment

Stitch
Mistletoe – slowly chew a berry

Teething of children
Orris root – chew

Warts
Greater celandine – apply juice to wart

Wound dressing
Sphagnum moss – apply to wounds

PERIWINKLE FAMILY **Periwinkles** The Lesser Periwinkle *Vinca minor* (**1**) and the Larger Periwinkle *V.
major* (**2**) are common garden plants, often found
naturalized in hedgerows and woodland. They both
make attractive ground cover plants and there are
white, pink and variegated types as well as blue. An
astringent prepared from the leaves can be used for
skin complaints, especially on the scalp. It also makes
a good mouthwash and was once believed to cure
diptheria. In Africa an extract of Periwinkle is a
traditional treatment for diabetes.

HOLLY FAMILY **Holly** *Ilex aquifolium* is a familiar bush or small tree, widespread in Europe, and there are many cultivars. Quite apart from its use as Christmas decorations, Holly is very versatile. Preparations of the bark help liver complaints while infusions and decoctions of the leaves were once used for digestive troubles, colic and malaria and were for some time the chief remedy for smallpox. Growing a holly bush in your garden is supposed to protect the house from lightning and witches. The berries can cause serious poisoning if eaten by children.

BORAGE FAMILY **Borage** *Borago officinalis* is a handsome addition to any herb garden. Borage can be grown from seed in March and will flower and grow vigorously all summer. A few leaves give a delicious cucumbery taste to summer drinks, iced tea, apple juice, soups and salad dressing. It is difficult to dry. Old herbals suggest adding borage to wine 'to make men glad and merrie'. It is used in various herbal remedies, especially for chest and throat complaints. Borage flowers can be frozen into ice cubes for long drinks.

Rough Comfrey *Symphytum asperum* is a large, vigorous herb covered in bristly hairs which is found in the wild in damp, shady places. It was once used as a compress on swellings, sprains and bruises. An infusion of leaves or flowers is useful for bronchial complaints and as an eyewash. Culpepper recommended taking it after accidents to help knit broken bones and the ground up roots were once used as a plaster. The leaves can be boiled like spinach and, fortunately for us, lose their hairiness when cooked.

NETTLE FAMILY **Hop** *Humulus lupulus* has been used in continental Europe for centuries to flavour beer and improve its keeping qualities. It became popular in English beer from the reign of Henry VIII. Hops have other beneficial effects, apart from their use in brewing. Hop tea calms the nerves and is said to cure worms and hops can be dried and stuffed into aromatic (if noisy) pillows to ease insomnia. The young shoots can be cooked and eaten. Hops are found naturalized in hedges and some garden varieties have attractive foliage.

Stinging Nettle *Urtica dioica* abounds almost everywhere, from mountains to sea level, in farmyards, woods and waste ground, and too often in our gardens. The fibrous stems have been used for coarse fabric, while the tops are delicious as a vegetable and in soup. Stout gloves must be worn to pick nettles, which lose their sting when cooked. Nettle tea soothes rheumatic pains and also makes a good hair rinse. The leaves give a green dye. Nettles are excellent butterfly plants. The seeds were once used as an aphrodisiac.

HONEYSUCKLE FAMILY **Elderberry** *Sambucus niger* is a common bush which graces hedges in June with an abundance of sweet-smelling, creamy flowers, which are delicious in cool drinks, cooked with gooseberries or eaten straight from the tree. Elderflower wine and 'champagne' have a wonderful bouquet, while the flower water helps sufferers from summer colds. The berries are good in apple pies and add a tartness to jams and jellies. The leaves, crushed up in water, can be used as a non-toxic, cheap herbal insecticide. Elderberry jam is a good laxative.

Guelder Rose *Viburnum opulus* is a large bush, common in woods and hedgerows. It has large clusters of fragrant flowers in June and the leaves turn a rich crimson in the autumn. The red berries are very unpleasant and emetic, if eaten raw, but when cooked can be made into cranberry-type sauce and are used in liqueurs. A drug derived from the bark relaxes the uterus and is given to alleviate various menopausal disturbances. It can also combat mild asthmatic attacks and relieve cramp.

PINK FAMILY **Carnations** and **Pinks** *Dianthus* spp. have been cultivated for centuries and all the scented ones can be dried for pot pourri. The clove-scented pink *D. caryophyllus* is easily grown from seed in spring, from cuttings or from layers in late summer. Though small, it has a suprisingly strong scent and the tips of the petals can be used to flavour puddings and custard or be added to milk shakes.

Soapwort *Saponaria officinalis* can often be found naturalized in single or double forms. The leaves and roots, when crushed in water, give a soapy lather which removes grease-spots from clothes. When mixed with an infusion of Rosemary it makes a fragrant shampoo which does not sting the eyes. The Romans put Soapwort in their baths to cure 'the itch' and other skin complaints and to soothe leprosy sores. Useful in the herb garden, Soapwort does not flower for long.

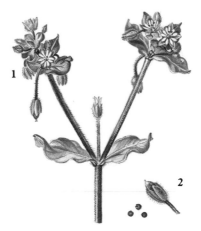

Pink Family (contd) **Chickweed** *Stellaria media* (**1**) is a familiar weed in hedgerows and gardens for most of the year. The soft, juicy stems and foliage make an interesting garnish and can be eaten like spinach. It was once applied as a hot poultice on boils and swellings. The whole plant, especially the seed pods (**2**) provides nutritious greenery for budgerigars, canaries and other pets. Gather early in the season for the kitchen – it is a favourite food plant for caterpillars. Chickweed soup with plenty of onions and pepper is very tasty, try it served with yoghurt.

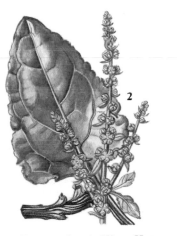

GOOSEFOOT FAMILY **Good King Henry** *Chenopodium bonus-henricus* (**1**), the only perennial British goosefoot, probably introduced by the Romans, is common throughout Europe on roadsides and waste places and as an agricultural weed. It is tastier than spinach and rich in iron.

Sea Beet *Beta vulgaris* ssp. *maritima* (**2**) is the ancestor of garden spinach, beetroot, sugar-beet and mangolds. It grows in estuaries and on shingle beaches all over Britain and on southern Atlantic coasts. It is delicious as a vegetable or in soups and flans.

GLASSWORT FAMILY **Marsh Samphire** *Salicornia europaea* This strange succulent plant grows on muddy salt-marshes, its odd stubby stems growing up to 30cm (1ft) tall. It is best gathered at midsummer and must always be well washed. The young plants can be eaten in salads or boiled and eaten with butter. Older plants can be pickled and used as a garnish. Samphire should be served with sea fish along with fennel and parsley sauce. Baked white fish with a samphire salad and a squeeze of lemon would make an excellent out-of-the-ordinary lunch for slimmers.

COMPOSITE FAMILY **Yarrow** *Achillea millefolium* is an attractive perennial that grows in grassy places all over Europe, with white, greyish or pink flowers. It has been used since ancient times to staunch wounds, especially on the battlefield, and to stop nosebleeds. More recently the leaves have been used in snuff and as a tobacco substitute. The leaves dry well and a tisane alleviates cold symptoms, brings down fevers and helps cramps. A decoction of Yarrow rubbed into the head is said to delay balding.

COMPOSITE FAMILY (contd) **Lesser Burdock** *Arctium minus* (**1**) and **Greater Burdock** *A. lappa* (**2**) are common on shady waste ground and in ditches throughout Europe, Lesser Burdock being a smaller plant. After a country walk the seed heads can often be found imbedded in one's socks. An extract of the whole plant is especially useful for skin complaints, eczema, acne, dandruff and boils: it stimulates the sebaceous and sweat glands. Young leaf stalks, peeled and boiled, make an interesting vegetable and can be eaten raw in salads. Fizzy dandelion and burdock was once as popular as modern cola drinks.

Daisy *Bellis perennis* is a common, pretty weed which pops up in lawns and gardens everywhere. Its pink and white flowers can often be seen throughout the year. Daisy roots are notoriously difficult to dig up, but the flat rosette of leaves can easily be weedkillered if it gets out of control. Extract of daisy can be taken as a tonic and expectorant and it is also anti-inflammatory. The young leaves add a spiciness to soup and salads and the flowers make an attractive garnish.

COMPOSITE FAMILY (contd) **Southernwood** or **Lad's Love** *Artemisia abrotanum* (**3**) is a must for every herb garden, it grows into an attractive aromatic bush, which should be clipped back in spring to keep it neat. The leaves have a delicious lemony scent and were once used for strewing. Sewn into muslin bags and hung in cupboards and placed in drawers it keeps clothes fresh while deterring moths. It makes a soporific tea which calms the nerves and the leaves, mixed with treacle, were once given to unfortunate children to cure worms.

Mugwort *A. vulgaris* (**2**) is common in the wild but tends to grow out of control in gardens. It is not as fragrant as Southernwood, but it is a better pot herb. The flowerheads render fatty meat, such as duck and goose, more digestible and were once used to flavour ale. The flowers are also a refreshing bath herb and, when drunk as a tisane, relieve rheumatism.

Wormwood *A. absinthium* (**1**) has very aromatic leaves and flowers and is used to flavour drinks, although absinthe is now prohibited in most countries. It is used medicinally in small doses as an anthelmintic, tonic and febrifuge, but can cause heart damage and hallucinations if taken in excess.

1

2

3

59

Composite Family (contd) **Tarragon** *Artemisia dracunculus* can be distinguished from the other *Artemisias* by its simple narrow, leaf. There are two common varieties. French tarragon is a slender bush needing winter protection and Russian tarragon is a tall hardy shrub. Both these varieties like a light, well-drained soil and can be propagated from cuttings, but the flowers seldom mature in the British climate. French tarragon is more difficult to grow but it is well worth the extra trouble. It has a sweet, peppery flavour, with a tang of liquorice, and should be used sparingly. Chop up young leaves and sprinkle on salads and fish, or add them to mayonnaise sauces and marinades. Tarragon is an essential ingredient in Bearnaise, Hollandaise and Tartare sauces. Russian tarragon can have an almost unbearably strong flavour and old bushes may have to be chopped back and transplanted to produce better-flavoured shoots. Tarragon does not dry well but a sprig in a bottle of olive oil or wine vinegar will bring freshness to winter salads. It was once applied to insect bites and stings and was thought to be particularly effective against dragons.

COMPOSITE FAMILY (contd) **Marigold** *Calendula officinalis* originates from India. It is annual and should be sown from seed in a sunny position. It will give a continuous supply of flowers until autumn if the dead heads are removed. The petals can be used fresh and keep well when dried. They give a spicy piquance to rice dishes, omelettes, fish and soups, and can be baked into cakes and buns. The petals also give a yellow dye similar to saffron. It is used in ointments for cuts, bruises, burns and sores. An infusion makes a soothing eyewash.

Blessed Thistle *Cnicus benedictus* is a yellow thistle, growing up to 1m (39in) tall, with reddish stems, originally from the Mediterranean. It was very common in medieval monastery gardens and sometimes still grows in their ruins. The whole plant is very bitter. Small doses of tisanes and tonics prepared from it stimulate the appetite and cure dyspepsia þut larger doses can cause unpleasant gastric upsets. The plant was once thought to have supernatural powers.

COMPOSITE FAMILY (contd) **Chicory** *Cichorium intybus*, with its fragile blue flowers, is commonly seen in waste places and roadsides on limey soil throughout Britain, Europe and the USA. It does not flower in the first year. The roots can be dried, roasted and added to coffee to give a mildly bitter taste. It is usually grown as a salad vegetable. Plants grown from seed in early spring can be lifted in autumn and forced in the dark to produce the 'chicons' or heads. There are many cultivars: red, white, curly, globe-shaped and outdoor ones that do

not need forcing. They all provided valuable winter salads and are suprisingly easy to grow. The chicons are also delicious baked in stock. An infusion of the leaves can be taken for depressive problems, or as a diuretic and bitter tonic. A poultice of leaves can be applied to boils and abscesses. A decoction mixed with wine is recommended by Culpepper for evil disposition of the body and long lingering agues.

COMPOSITE FAMILY (contd) **Globe Artichoke** *Cynara scolymus*, the wild artichoke from which all cultivated ones were developed, comes from southern Europe and North Africa. It can be propagated by division and easily grows quite large. The flowerheads make a delicious starter if cut just before they open, boiled for 30-40 minutes and served with butter or a herby dressing. The floral bracts are stripped off successively and the base of each eaten until you reach the succulent heart. A bitter extract of the leaves is a liver tonic and diuretic and is used in skin preparations.

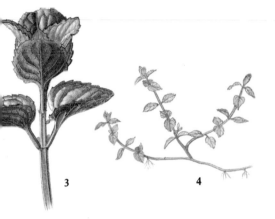

3   4

All the mints are excellent appetisers and digestives and have been popular for centuries. Mint oil is antiseptic, relieves colds and eases toothache. In the kitchen mints are indispensible – for mint sauce on lamb, chopped on to potatoes and salads, in yoghurt and puddings or in hot and cold drinks. Mint tea is an ideal drink after any meal. If you see the orangey-brown spots of mint rust on the leaves harvest them all immediately and propagate in the autumn from the runners. through which the fungus cannot be carried.

LABIATE FAMILY (contd) **Basil** *Ocimum basilicum* is a delicate annual herb originating from India (where it is perennial). It is not easy to grow but is well worth a little trouble. Given warmth and shelter it will form a nice bushy plant. In cold climates it can be grown from seed each year in a pot outside, but take it indoors in cold, wet weather. It is an ideal kitchen windowsill herb and will even deter flies. The leaves bruise easily and should be dried slowly in the dark. The Indians use it in curries and in Europe it is the typical herb of spaghetti, pizza and tomato dishes. It is also delicious with sausages, cheese and fish, or sprinkled on tomato or potato soup. Oil of Basil is used in perfumery and is supposed to clear headaches and have a laxative and sedative action. The leaves are also an ingredient of snuff. Bush Basil is hardier, more compact and has less flavour.

LABIATE FAMILY **Oregano** or **Wild Marjoram** *Origanum vulgare* (**1**) is one of the oldest herbs in use today. It grows on chalky hillsides as a leafy bush with creeping stems and has a variable flavour. It is much used in Spanish, Italian and Mexican cooking. Once established it makes a good garden plant.

Sweet Marjoram *O. majorana* (**2**) was introduced into Britain by the Romans. It is a bushy annual which must be protected from frost and grows well in pots and windowboxes. It has a sweet, subtle flavour and is used in sausages, hamburgers and pizza. It also acts as a disinfectant and preservative.

Pot Marjoram *O. monites* (**3**) is a hardy perennial and grows wild in Sicily. It has less flavour than Sweet marjoram but is an easier plant to grow. It has tall flowering stems and spreads rapidly, so it must be kept trimmed.

The leaves of all marjorams can be collected from July-September in the northern hemisphere. Their flavour improves on drying. The marjorams are very good bee plants, there are a great many different species, some with attractive foliage.

124

LABIATE FAMILY (contd) **Rosemary** *Rosmarinus officinalis* A bush of Rosemary is essential in every herb garden. Rosemary originates from hot, dry rocky hillsides in the Mediterranean, so if grown in colder climates should be protected from frost. It flourishes best in a light, sandy, dry soil with a little lime and plenty of sun, reaching up to 1.5m (5ft), and once established it will be there for years. There are several varieties, the smallest *R. prostrata* grows up to 20cm (8in) and has dark purple flowers.

Rosemary can be propagated from cuttings, seeds or layers. It has a spicy, piney, gingery taste and smell and can be used as an air freshener or as a moth repellent. Rosemary tea is very therapeutic, especially for stomach complaints, and was used by the Greeks to improve the memory. Rosemary is excellent with roast chicken or game and also in jams, custards and biscuits. A leg of lamb with a Rosemary and Garlic stuffing is quite delicious. Rosemary oil is used in perfumery and is a pleasant-smelling antiseptic.

LABIATE FAMILY (contd) **Sage** *Salvia officinalis* There are an enormous number of different sages, all with aromatic properties. The familiar broad-leaved English Sage (**1**) grows into a bush 60cm (2ft) tall and likes a light chalky soil in a dry sunny position. It has a very good flavour and dries well. One plant is sufficient for most households, so choose your bush carefully, you will have it for years.

Dwarf, Variegated (**2**) and 'Pineapple' Sage (**3**) are best for tubs and windowboxes but they must be kept trimmed and replaced by cuttings if they get too leggy, or they will take over. **Purple Sage** *S. officinalis* 'Purpurascens' (**4**) has very attractive leaves and will give an unusual patch of colour in the herb garden.

Sage has a strong flavour and sage tea was once used for a universal cure-all as it helps all gastric upsets, has antiseptic properties and is good for mouth infections. It can be used sparingly in cheeses and herb butter and to flavour pickles. Traditional Sage and Onion stuffing should always accompany roast chicken or turkey and will make even a bland modern bird taste special.

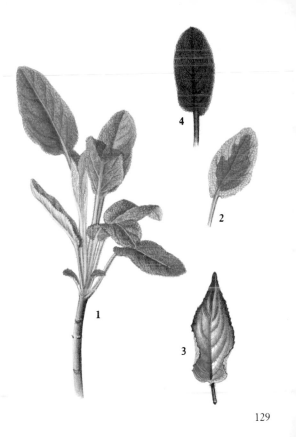

129

LABIATE FAMILY (contd) **Winter Savory** *Satureja montana* (**1**) is a small perennial, evergreen shrub, growing in a compact bush. It likes a poor, limey soil in a sunny, well-drained position and once established is easy to keep. It can be grown from seed outside in April (in the northern hemisphere) or from 15cm (6in) cuttings taken in March or April. The cuttings can be planted 15cm (6in) apart in the back of the border. Transplant rooted cuttings in September. The leaves are better used fresh, as they become rather tough on drying, but if the plant is protected from frost it will give fresh leaves all the year round. It has a stronger flavour then Summer Savory and is good in bouquet garni, otherwise it has similar uses. There are both upright and creeping varieties.

Summer Savory *S. hortensis* (**2**) is an annual, more delicate than Winter Savory but with a much more subtle spicy, fragrant, savory flavour. It grows into a tender bush and likes a sunny position and rich soil. Seed should be sown in April in a light poor soil in a sunny position and grows well in window boxes. The leaves can be cut for cooking as required but for drying should be cut before the plant flowers. It is an antiflatulent and is therefore recommended for all bean dishes and in cucumber salads. It is very good in pork sausages, pork pies and stuffings. A sprig of savory added to boiling cauliflower or sprouts will keep the smells down. Both savories are good bee plants.

LABIATE FAMILY (contd) **Betony** or **Woundwort**
Stachys officinalis grows wild on heaths, in hedges and
open woods throughout Britain and Europe. It was
once considered a holy herb, used to deter visions,
bad dreams, witches and possession by devils, and
thought to be essential for killing serpents. The name
Woundwort derives from its more usual function as
a dressing for sores and ulcers. This versatile herb
was also effective against worms and breathlessness.
The dried leaves can make a tea-like infusion which
soothes headaches and they can also be made into
tobacco and snuff.

Wall Germander *Teucrium chamaedrys* is an attractive little herb, growing wild in dry places all over Europe. In medieval times it was used to treat dropsy, jaundice and gout, but nowadays it is more in demand as a flavouring for Chartreuse liqueur. A tisane made from the flowering tops quietens an upset stomach and can be taken for liver troubles, anaemia and bronchitis. If the crushed plant is applied to sores and ulcers it will reduce inflammations and encourage the healing process.

LABIATE FAMILY (contd) **Wild Thyme** *Thymus sarpyllum* (**1**) grows commonly on grassy heaths and downs of northern Europe, giving off a wonderful smell of incense on sunny days, and there are many other thymes. Thymes like a well-drained, sunny, open position and limey soil. They can be grown from layers or cuttings and can be potted up for indoor winter use.

Garden Thyme *T. vulgare* (**2**) is more bushy and aromatic than Wild Thyme and has an enormous variety of uses. A tisane of Thyme was once used to prevent giddiness and nightmares and bunches were burned to fumigate houses and repel insects. It has also been used for gastric upsets and bronchial

troubles. Thymol extract is now found in throat pastilles, mouthwash, toothpaste and bath oil. Thyme aids the digestion of fatty meats, such as mutton and pork, and is very good in cottage and cream cheese and in bouquets garnis as it dries easily. Thyme soup was once used as a cure for shyness!

Lemon thyme *T. citriodorus* (**3**) has a warm lemon scent and is used in perfumery. It is a good bee plant and gives their honey a delicious flavour.

Among the other varieties there are creeping, upright and large-leaved types with flowers coloured from white to deep purple. **Variegated Thyme** (**4**) makes an attractive edging plant.

LAUREL FAMILY **Bay** *Laurus nobilis* can be grown into a handsome, evergreen tree up to 20cm (60ft) tall, often found growing as an escape in woods and wastelands outside its native range. It can easily be kept as a standard bush or, if trimmed, is suitable for small pots in window boxes and on patios. Bay is difficult to grow from seed but cuttings should root if taken in early summer and kept in a moist atmosphere. It is often found in large gardens, trimmed into ornamental shapes but is seldom seen nowadays in laurel wreaths, being more popular for its culinary uses. The leaves can be picked and dried throughout the year and add a distinctive flavour to bouquet garnis, preserves, marinades, soups and stews, especially beef dishes. the leaves can also be baked in milk to flavour rice puddings or sauces in place of vanilla. The dried leaves have a better, sweeter flavour than fresh ones. The leaves contain a volatile oil that can be rubbed into rheumatic joints and is made into Laurin ointment. A decoction of the leaves works as a general stimulant and helps settle gastric upsets.

Warning: Do not confuse with the Spurge laurel *Daphne laureola* of gardens, which is poisonous.

137

PEA FAMILY **Liquorice** *Glycyrrhiza glabra* We must all be familiar with such confectionery as Pontefract cakes and liquorice bootlaces, but few will have seen the plant responsible for them. It is a perennial herb, growing up to 1m (3½ft) high, with a large root system and long horizontal stolons, cultivated all over Europe and in America. Liquorice is extracted from the roots and stolons. It is propagated from divisions of the stolons in spring, in rows 60-90cm (2-3ft) apart. The foliage should be cut down every autumn and side stolons removed for three successive years. It is then ready for harvesting. It was used by the ancient Chinese, Greeks and Egyptians for throat complaints, heartburn and as a wound dressing. Liquorice is very sweet and viscous and is useful in cough medicines and pastilles and as an expectorant. It is also rich in vitamin B. Liquorice dissolved in milk soothes colds and catarrh, and a 'flu victim should never be without a few liquorice sticks. It is also used for colouring shoe polish.

138

139

PEA FAMILY **Sweet Pea** *Lathyrus odoratus* has a
dreamy scent and flowers should be carefully dried in
the dark for pot pourri. The wild species (**1a**) has the
better scent but smaller flowers than cultivated ones
(**1b**). Sweet peas are easily grown from seed and can
be trained up pea-sticks at the back of the herb
garden.

Restharrow *Ononis spinosa* (**2**) is a much-branched
spiny undershrub, up to 30cm (1ft) tall, growing in
rough dry grassland, with very long roots that were
reputed to break farm implements, hence the name.
An infusion of the roots is diuretic and was used by

140

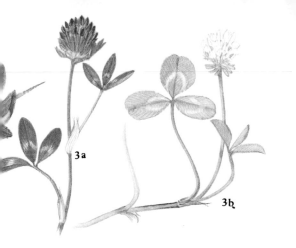

3a

3b

the Romans to dissolve kidney stones and for urinary disorders; the young roots can be cooked and eaten as a vegetable.

Clovers *Trifolium pratense* (**3a**) and *T. repens* (**3b**) are abundant throughout Britain and Europe in grassy places, are often sown for pasture and are common on weedy lawns. An infusion of red clover was used for whooping cough and bronchitis and as a poultice on nasty tumours. The dried flowers make a tisane and fresh flowers can be eaten in salads and sandwiches. Clovers, particularly white clover, are very popular with bees and British clover honey is justly famous.

141

LILY FAMILY **Onion** *Allium cepa* (**1**) is a biennial herb, producing a large bulb in its first year and flowering in the second year. Easily grown from seed, or more conveniently from 'sets' (baby onions). Onions were widely used by both the Romans and the Egyptians and were probably around long before either. There are many varieties, colours, shapes and sizes. Apart from their culinary properties, onions have been hung over doors to avert plague and, more recently, foot and mouth disease. A drug derived from the bulbs is a disinfectant, helps catarrh and soothes sore eyes and earache. Eaten in quantity, onions are supposed to ward off colds, induce sleep, cure indigestion and prevent arteriosclerosis. Onion skins make a strong brown-to-yellow dye.

Shallots *A. ascalonicum* (**2**) are attractive, small-sized bulbs which grow in clusters. They have a milder flavour than onions and can be added whole to stews and casseroles. Onions and shallots can be tied up in bunches for winter use. A few shallots can be kept for planting out the following spring.

142

1

2

LILY FAMILY (contd) **Chives** *Allium schoenoprasum* is native in northern Europe and can occasionally be found wild on limestone cliffs near fresh water. The plants grow easily from root divisions and, if developing flowerhead are removed, will provide a supply of leaves from spring to autumn. The taste is milder and less persistent than onions and very good in soft cheeses, soups or as a garnish. The plant is rich in iron and volatile oils and is a good appetizer for invalids. It will also reduce the blood pressure and strengthen the heart. Chives do not dry easily.

Welsh Onion *Allium fistulosum* or Onion Green probably originated in east Asia. It has a stronger flavour than Chives and the hollow leaves, sliced, make an attractive garnish. It is a hardy perennial and, unlike Chives, is available throughout the winter. It does not dry well. the 'roots' can easily be divided up to give new plants. It makes a very good bread sauce.

1

LILY FAMILY (contd) **Garlic** *Allium sativum* (**1**) is not found in the wild but has been used for centuries. The Romans used it to cure worms and as a diuretic, as well as for cooking. The bulbs yield a stimulant, bring down fevers and ease bronchial conditions. Modern pharmacologists confirm that garlic is a vasco-dilator and has potential for the treatment of arteriosclerosis. It is rich in vitamins, adds a special flavour to salad dressings and marinades and can be used in many meat dishes, sausages, pate, soups and stews. Unfortunately it stays

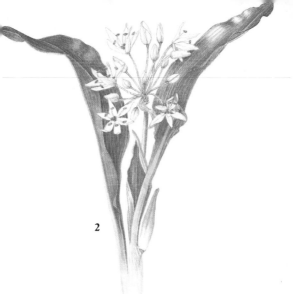

2

on the breath for some time after eating it. Garlic is easily propagated by planting out separate 'cloves' in a light sunny position.

Ramsons *A. ursinium* (**2**) is found by its pervasive smell, flowering in damp woods and hedges throughout Europe in early summer. Its star-like flowers are very attractive but their smell makes them unsuitable for vases in the house. It is more subtle than garlic and most of the flavour goes when cooked.

LILY FAMILY **Autumn Crocus** *Colchicum autumnale* is also called Naked Ladies or Meadow Saffron (from its habit of flowering before the leaves appear). It is not a true crocus and is poisonous to humans and livestock. It grows throughout Europe and North Africa but is rarely seen wild in Britain today. The corms and seeds are used for the extraction of Colchicine which has been used since early times as an eyewash and is still used in Homeopathy as an eyewash and astringent. Colchicine is used by geneticists and plant breeders to cause mutations in cell chromosomes.

148

Lily of the Valley *Convallaria majalis* is an attractive, very sweet-smelling plant of shady woods around the world and is commonly grown in gardens. Its flowers are excellent in pot pourri. It produces a drug similar to Digitalis, but milder and not cumulative, used as a heart stimulant and diuretic. A preparation of the plant in wine was claimed to restore speech after a stroke. Gerard buried phials of flowers in ants' nests and later applied them to gouty feet.

149

FLAX FAMILY **Flax** or **Linseed** *Linum usitatissimum* is an annual originating in southern Europe with delicate, blue flowers. There are tall varieties, the stem fibres of which are made into linen, and varieties with high seed-oil content which give linseed oil. The seeds are very mucilaginous and highy efficient laxatives are prepared from them. The same preparation can be applied as a poultice to boils and abscesses. Linseed oil is an essential ingredient in nutritious bran mash fed to horses, which is poisonous if not properly prepared.

MISTLETOE FAMILY **Mistletoe** *Viscum album* is
semi-parasitic, different types growing on apple,
poplar, lime and other trees, and dispersed by birds
eating the berries. It is found all over Europe and
cultivated for Christmas decorations in apple or-
chards. The Druids considered it magical and only
cut it with a golden sickle. They used it to treat
epilepsy for which it is still used today. A drug
prepared from the leaves and branches is antispasmodic and diuretic and is also given for
hypertension and arteriosclerosis. A ripe berry,
quietly chewed, is said to cure the stitch.

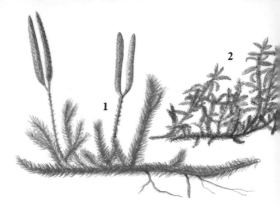

CLUBMOSS FAMILY **Clubmoss** *Lycopodium clavatum* (**1**) is not a true moss but grows in mossy places on heaths and moors in northern Europe and is very distinctive with low, creeping stems and tiny rows of leaves. It is diuretic and used for various urinary afflictions. The spores, which are produced in clouds, contain a high proportion of essential oils and are quite inflammable – they are very light and easily blown about, ideal for making theatrical explosions. They are also added to snuff.

SPHAGNUM FAMILY **Sphagnum Moss** *Sphagnum cymbifolium* (**2**) grows in boggy places. A true moss, well-known for its water-retaining and bactericidal properties, it is ideal for lining baskets and packing cuttings and plants for transport. Before the advent of

modern antiseptics and sterile dressings it was commonly used to dress wounds.

LOOSESTRIFE FAMILY **Purple Loosestrife** *Lythrum salicaria* is a large herb, growing in ditches, marshes and on riverbanks all over northern Europe, flowering from June to August. Gerard valued it as a remedy for eye infections and 'blows and hurts' to the eyes. An infusion of the flowering tops can relieve diarrhoea and was once used, probably with little success, to dye the hair blonde. The plant can be burnt and waved about to deter mosquitoes and biting insects. The Romans wove Loosestrife into garlands and hung them around the necks of their oxen to quieten them.

MALLOW FAMILY This family contains several pretty and beneficial herbs. **Mallow** *Malva sylvestris* (**1**) and **Marsh Mallow** *Althaéa officinals* (**2**) grow quite tall, up to 1m (3¼ft) and look good at the back of a herb border. Marsh Mallow has a liking for boggy places, Mallow grows wild at roadsides and on waste land and the other Mallows like a well-drained soil, a sunny position and protection from winter rain. They can be grown easily from seed or from cuttings taken in late autumn. Culpepper used Mallows as the universal cure-all, preparations of the leaves being given for coughs, sore throats and digestive complaints as well as for gonorrhoea and toothache. The flowers make a soothing herb tea and the roots were made into ointment for chapped hands and chilblains. The roots of the Marsh Mallow contain starch and albumen and are very gelatinous - they were used to make the familiar marshmallow sweets (nowadays made from gelatine).

Dwarf Mallow *Malva rotundifolia* (**3**) has similar properties and the young leaves and flowers can be eaten in salads.

1

2

3

MALLOW FAMILY (contd) **Hollyhock** *Althaea rosea* is a common garden plant, often escaping and growing along walls, in wasteland and dry places. There are double and single types and many colour forms. It has similar properties to the other mallows. Culpepper used it to prevent miscarriage and to treat worms. It is a very attractive plant, typical of cottage gardens, but unfortunately susceptible to rust fungus.

BOGBEAN FAMILY **Bogbean** *Menthyanthes trifoliata* is
an odd-looking plant, not often seen in the wild, as it
grows in very marshy conditions and rather inaccess-
ible places. It can be grown in ornamental ponds but
with its long creeping rhizomes must be kept in
check. The flowers and leaves have been made into
infusions for feverish colds since antiquity. In small
doses it is a laxative and aids and stimulates the
digestion, but in larger doses it is purgative and
emetic.

157

OLIVE FAMILY **Ash** *Fraxinus excelsior* grows as a handsome tall tree throughout Europe. The timber is very strong and springy and used for chairlegs and broomsticks. The bark was once made into tonics for rheumatism and liver complaints, the fruits were eaten to cure flatulence. An infusion of ash leaves is a mild laxative and has long been recommended as a cure for overweight. Ash keys (the fruits) can be pickled: they must first be boiled, changing the water twice, to remove bitterness.

WOOD SORREL FAMILY **Wood Sorrel** *Oxalis acetosella* is a pretty creeping plant, common throughout Europe in woods and shady places, with distinctive trefoil leaves and nodding pinkish bell-shaped flowers. It is not particularly useful as a herb but brightens up the garden in April and May when there is not much colour about. A few leaves can be eaten in salads and in white sauce or mayonnaise it sharpens the flavour. It is poisonous in large doses

POPPY FAMILY **Greater Celandine** *Chelidonium majus* is found in spring in hedgerows and around old buildings. It was grown extensively as a medicinal herb: its yellow, acrid, sticky juice has a nasty smell and many uses. It was made into a purgative and digestive aid and, in more dilute form, an eye lotion. A large dose can be fatal. The sticky sap will remove warts and will soften corns, if you can bear the smell. It was used in Elizabethan times to loosen teeth before extraction.

160

Fumitory *Fumaria officinalis* is a delicate common weed, often found in dry stony places and growing out of old walls. Its greyish filmy leaves were thought by the Romans to spring from the ground without seeds, like mist. They used it to drive off melancholy and as a general tonic. It has diuretic and aperitif effects and can be used as a treatment against worms. It was once used in various skin preparations and to remove freckles.

161

POPPY FAMILY (contd) **Corn Poppy** *Papaver rhoeas* (**1**) grows commonly all over the temperate zones of the world in verges and on wasteland and as a weed of cultivation. There are numerous garden varieties of this attractive annual plant, which seeds itself readily each year. It does not contain morphine. The juice has been used for centuries as a mild sedative and was once mixed into babies' porridge. A drug made from the dried petals is used to help children with whooping cough and bronchitis. The seeds have a peppery nuttiness and are delicious on bread and cakes, mixed with honey, as a filling for pastries or cooked with macaroni or rice dishes. Poppyseed oil is expensive but add a little to French dressings and mayonnaise.

Opium Poppy *P. somniferum* (**2**) produces a juice, in hot climates, from which opium and morphine can be extracted. It has been cultivated for centuries and there are many garden varieties. It is a very handsome plant and can be grown from seed. The seeds do not contain the drug and can be used in cooking like those of the Corn Poppy. The seed oil is used by artists in paint and varnish.

162

1

2

163

PLANTAIN FAMILY **Ribwort** *Plantago lanceolata* There
are several species of plantain with similar medicinal
properties. They are commonly found in grassy
places and the tough, perennial rosette of leaves is
often seen in garden paths and lawns. The seeds
contain up to ten per cent mucilage and, made into a
jelly with water or chewed whole, will sooth gut
irritations and cure constipation. Preparations of the
seeds can also be taken for dysentry. Culpepper
recommended it for 'all torments and excoriations of
the intestines'. An infusion of the leaves was taken by
Alexander the Great to cure headache, it is also
effective against toothache and earache. The young
leaves are very tasty in salads.

DOCK FAMILY **Bistort** *Polygonum bistorta* is widespread and locally common in wet, hill pastures of northern latitudes. It is easily grown from root divisions and likes a shady spot. The leaves make a tasty vegetable or salad and were once the basic ingredient of an Easter pudding, along with Nettle tops, Dandelion leaves and Lady's Mantle. This, like Yorkshire pudding, was eaten with meat. A decoction of the dried roots can be used as a mouthwash or as a gargle for sore throats. Powdered roots were once made into bread.

Dock Family (contd) **Water Pepper** *Polygonum hydropiper* is a common inconspicuous annual growing in ditches and damp places throughout Europe. It has a very bitter taste and animals will not eat it. An infusion of the leaves was once taken to dissolve kidney stones and it was applied as a poultice to varicose veins. It is astringent and can be used in face preparations to close enlarged pores. An infusion of the whole plant, poured into a fragrant herbal bath, relieves rheumatic aches and pains.

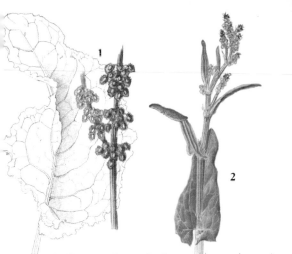

Dock *Rumex crispus* (**1**) is a widespread weed throughout Europe. The large dark green leaves were once eaten as a vegetable but are rather bitter. They spice up a ham omlette. A dock leaf rubbed on to a child's nettle sting seems to give immediate relief – this sometimes works on adults too.

Sorrel *R. acetosa* (**2**) is widespread and common in grassland throughout Europe. It is prized as a vegetable in France and there are cultivated forms. The young leaves are sharp and refreshing in salads, soups and omelettes, and make a very good cold soup with yoghurt.

DOCK FAMILY (contd) **Rhubarb** *Rheum raponticum* is surely familiar to everyone. Most old gardens will have it and, if yours does not, beg a piece of root off a neighbour, plant it in a deep rich soil and it will be there for years. Leaf stalks can be cut in early summer, or forced under straw or a 'rhubarb bell' for an earlier crop. Rhubarb originated in Tibet and was grown in monastery gardens all over Europe for its mild astringent and purgative actions. The powdered root can be taken for stomach and bowel troubles. The stalks are delicious stewed with sugar, in pies, tarts and puddings. Slimmers can use Sweet Cecily roots and leaves to replace some of the sugar. Rhubarb is very acidic, so much so that it will descale kettles. The leaves are very poisonous to humans, and to aphids. Simmer two or three leaves in a little water, strain and dilute to 1 litre (2 pints) and add a few drops of washing up liquid to make an inexpensive herbal insecticide which should be used fresh.

169

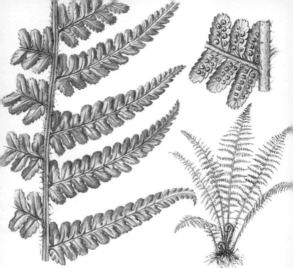

FERN FAMILY **Male Fern** *Dryopteris felix-mas* is often found in shady damp woods and banks throughout the temperate zone. It was recognized in early times as an efficient cure for worms. The dried rhizome was ground up and mixed with honey for tapeworm or with wine and barley for the less tenacious types. These treatments were too powerful for children to take. The rhizome can be cut up and boiled in water to give a soft green dye. Male Fern has delicate autumn colour and is very attractive in flower arrangements.

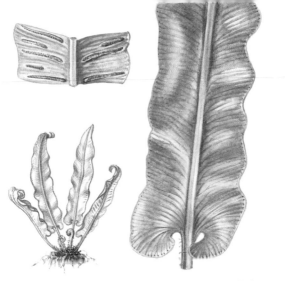

Hartstongue *Phyllitis scolopendrium* is a very distinctive fern growing in damp shady places and is often seen growing down wells and in rock fissures throughout the British Isles and in many parts of Europe. The large leaves contain mucilage and can be made into an expectorant infusion to ease bronchial catarrh. The infusion was once used for extreme cases of 'passion of the heart' and was also though to make people invisible – because the flowers were apparently invisible. It was also taken as a cure for hiccoughs.

FERN FAMILY (contd) **Polypody** or **Wood Liquorice**
Polypodium vulgare is found in shady places on walls,
cliffs and at the foot of old trees all over Europe and
the Mediterranean region. The tufted, creeping
rhizome smells of liquorice, but it is rather bitter. The
plant is purgative and can be given to patients with
chronic constipation. Like the Male Fern it cures
worms. As ferns produce spores under the fronds,
instead of flowering and producing seed, for centuries
they were thought to flower in secret when no-one
was looking.

BUTTERCUP FAMILY **Pheasant's Eye** *Adonis vernalis* (**1**) is a herbaceous perennial from the mountainous regions of France, Spain and central Europe. It can make a very attractive, if not very useful, addition to the herb garden. Drugs obtained from Pheasant's Eye were once used as a local anaesthetic and early herbalists used it for treating dropsy. It has properties similar to *Digitalis* and can be used to reduce swellings due to heart conditions.

Summer Adonis *A. annua* (**2**) has a similar action and can occasionally be found in weedy cornfields.

BUTTERCUP FAMILY (contd) **Columbine** *Aquilega vulgaris* This pretty perennial herb, commonly grown in our gardens, is found wild in woods in Europe. There are blue, pink, white and bi-coloured forms which readily seed themselves between other plants. Extracts of the leaves were once a useful home remedy for sore throats. Columbine was popular in Germany for treating swollen glands and to relieve palpitations of the heart. The fresh juice can be applied to ulcers and boils to promote healing.

Rose Family **Agrimony** *Agrimonia eupatoria*, a common plant in grass verges and meadows, has been used for centuries for eye treatments and was once supposed to cure cataracts. An infusion of the leaves and flowers can make a breath freshener and mouthwash and is reputedly good for the liver – a useful 'morning-after' remedy. It was used by the Anglo-Saxons to remove warts and to treat snakebite. In France it is still recommended as a cure for bed-wetting.

Rose Family (contd) **Lady's Mantle** *Alchemilla vulgaris* grows in grassy places in most areas of Europe. The hairy leaves are especially attractive in the morning dew. It is perennial, and can be grown easily from seed, but must be cut back or it may become a nuisance. The dried leaves make a useful tea for all female complaints. Culpepper recommended an infusion of the leaves to restore the figure after confinements. It can be applied to skin inflammations and acne and makes a soothing bath herb.

176

Hawthorn *Crataegus monogyna* is a common small tree in older hedgerows. The pink or white blossom gives off an interesting musky scent – too strong for indoor arrangements. The leaves make a sedative tisane. The young leaves can be eaten in sandwiches and salads, they have a fresh, nutty taste. The fruits, or haws, appear in autumn; they can be chewed raw but are best made into jelly with crab apples. An infusion of haws will help to draw out thorns and splinters. A drug derived from the haws is useful for nervous disorders, hypertension, menopausal upsets and dropsy. It is also soporific. Soak the haws in brandy to make a good liqueur.

ROSE FAMILY **Meadowsweet** *Filipendula ulmaria* can be found in damp meadows and ditches, its creamy yellow flowers giving off a heady scent all summer. It was used as an aromatic strewing herb and a flavouring for mead and beer. The whole plant is soothing to the stomach and bowel, and with honey makes a handy mild remedy for children's diarrhoea. An infusion soothes rheumatism and will also help cure skin eruptions. Meadowsweet flowers are excellent in pot pourri. The flowers, mixed with rose petals and thyme, will make very sweet-smelling herb bags for scenting clothes and linen.

178

Wild Strawberry *Fragaria vesca* has very sweet, tasty,
if seedy fruits which can be found in woodland
clearings and grassland, usually on limey soils. It is
very pretty to grow and a few small fruits are
interesting on top of strawberry desserts. The crushed
fruits are an age-old remedy for removing freckles.
They are also a delicious way to whiten stained teeth.
An infusion of the leaves will bring down fevers and
can be used as a gargle. The leaves make a good tisane
but do not dry well. There are a great many cultivated
varieties, some with giant fruits, some fruiting in
autumn.

179

Rose Family (contd) **Wood Avens** or **Herb Bennet**
Geum urbanum is a short, humble plant, growing in
shady places under hedges and in woodland. The
roots have a pleasant clove-like taste and smell and
were once used to repel moths and flavour ale. A
digestive tonic was made from the roots and was said
to cure general debility if taken regularly for several
months. The leaves add an unusual flavour to soups
and stews. It was thought to repel biting insects.

Silverweed *Potentilla anserina* abounds in damp, grassy places and is often a garden weed. It would be very attractive if it were not so persistent. The silvery, hairy leaves were used as a comfy boot-lining for footsore travellers. The roots were baked or boiled and eaten before potatoes were introduced into Europe. They can also be chewed raw, like carrots, or dried and ground into a flour for bread or for thickening soups and gruel.

181

ROSE FAMILY (contd) **Common Tormentil** *Potentilla erecta* is common on heathland, moors and mountains. It has a thick, perennial rhizome. A decoction of the roots is similar to oil of cloves and eases toothache and it can be applied to children's gums to help cutting teeth. A tisane of the leaves can be taken for gastric upsets and diarrhoea, it is also a tonic and will reduce fevers. The roots have been used in traditional remedies for haemorrhoids and frostbite. They also give a red dye and can be gathered in the spring or autumn and dried in the sun for use later.

Salad Burnet *Sanguisorba minor* is a pretty perennial herb found in chalky grassland. It can be easily grown in window boxes as an annual. Seeds can be sown in autumn or spring, in sun or semi-shade, and need plenty of moisture in the growing season. It can also be propagated from root division in spring. It gives a continuous supply of fresh leaves if the flowers are cut off. The young leaves have a cucumbery taste, delicious in a salad or as a garnish. It is also good in summer drinks, soups and mayonnaise. The Greeks added it to wine to cheer the heart and drive off melancholy.

ROSE FAMILY (contd) **Sloe** *Prunus spinosa* abounds in hedges throughout Britain, France and Germany. Its delicate white blossom, Blackthorn, is a sure sign that spring is on its way. Sloes (the fruit) should be gathered after the first frost. Sloe jelly, an excellent accompaniment to meat dishes, is made from sloes, crab apples, cinnamon, cloves, allspice and brown sugar. There are many closely-guarded recipes for slow gin – but if you pack sloes, gin, orange peel, cinnamon, sugar and whatever else you like into a wide-necked jar and seal for six months, then strain it, you should find the results quite interesting.

184

Dog Rose *Rosa canina* can be seen flowering in most north temperate hedgerows in May and June. Its delicate pink petals, which fall soon after picking, are made into rosewater and dried for pot pourri. The hips should be collected in autumn after the first frosts. They are twenty times richer in vitamin C than oranges and rose hip syrup is very good for children and invalids. The hips make good jams and jellies. Rose hip tea is beneficial to the gall bladder and kidneys. The very hairy pips are a highly effective substitute for itching powder, the hairs are difficult to remove from clothing.

ROSE FAMILY **Blackberry** *Rubus fruticosus* flourishes wild all over the Old and New Worlds. There are many species and varieties and the taste and size of berries is variable. There are many garden varieties, even thornless ones, but these are only worth growing if you cannot find them wild. An ancient remedy for boils was to crawl backwards through a blackberry thicket: it is doubtful whether this helped the boils but patients would certainly feel better when they stopped. Gerard recommended Blackberry lotion for sores of the mouth and 'secret parts'. The berries are quite delicious in apple pies and as a flavouring in drinks. Blackberries in vinegar are a traditional cure for sore throats.

Raspberry *Rubus idaeus* can be widely found in woods and in cultivation all over Europe. It is best grown in full sun, in a well-drained soil. Raspberries are very rich in vitamins B and C. An infusion of the leaves is very tasty and can be used as a gargle. The boiled leaves give a drug which relieves labour pains and is a mild laxative. The fruits are unarguably the most delicious of such fruits and there are many cultivated types.

BEDSTRAW FAMILY **Woodruff** *Galium odoratum* can be found covering the ground in dark woods and hedgerows in the spring. Culpepper gave Woodruff extracts to consumptives and used it as an aphrodisiac. The whorls of leaves can be pulled off and dried flat, they smell strongly of new-mown hay and are a mild sedative. Traditional 'May Wine' is made by adding sugar, Woodruff, Strawberries and a little sherry to a bottle of hock – leave to steep for an hour and strain before drinking. The whorls of dried leaves are ideal for scenting a pile of handkerchiefs.

Cleavers or **Goosegrass** *Galium aparine* is frequently found clinging to one's clothing after country walks. It grows abundantly in hedgerows, woods and waste places throughout Europe, sprawling over the other plants. Like Woodruff it is mildly sedative and soothing. The crushed herb was applied as a poultice on sores and ulcers, and the juice of the leaves used to staunch bleeding. It can be eaten as a spring vegetable and Goosegrass broth was once taken to cure overweight. The fruits can be roasted and ground into a coffee substitute. The roots give a red to yellow dye.

BEDSTRAW FAMILY (contd) **Madder Root** *Rubia tinctoria* was used by the ancient Egyptians to dye cotton cloth. It can be grown from seed sown in spring or autumn and likes a deep, rich soil and a sunny position. Alizarin crimson dye and various madder pigments varying from rose to brown and purple were originally made from the roots but they are now made chemically. It was once applied to the face to remove freckles – possibly by dyeing the rest of the face darker!

RUE FAMILY **Rue** *Ruta graveolens* was introduced into Britain by the Romans. The blue-grey leaves give off a distinctive smell. It is supposed to grow better if stolen from another garden but is associated with a great power against evil. It was used in nosegays to keep off plague and evil spirits and taken as an antidote to all deadly poisons. A preparation of Rue, Figs and honey was applied to the knees and the feet to prevent gout and dropsy. It was also supposed to preserve chastity – there is no evidence that it was effective.

FIGWORT FAMILY **Foxglove** *Digitalis purpurea*
is undoubtedly one of the most handsome wild
plants. It grows in hedges, woods and on
heathland throughout Britain and western
Europe. There are many garden varieties
which look impressive at the back of any
herbaceous border. The drug digitalis has
been used in the treatment of heart conditions
since the seventeenth century. It is very
powerful and accumulative so should only be
used on prescription. The leaves can be used
as a poultice on sprained joints.

Eyebright *Euphrasia officinalis* is a semi-parasitic annual, common in a variety of places. It has been used for centuries in remedies for the eyes. Herbalists make it into an eye lotion to bathe the eyes, or it can be taken internally to cure conjunctivitis. It is astringent and reduces inflammation. The whole plant can be made into an eye compress. Eyebright tea aids the digestion and it is good for the gall bladder.

FIGWORT FAMILY (contd) **Toadflax** *Linaria vulgaris* is a pretty wayside plant of late summer. Extracts of the plant are powerfully diuretic and 'doth somewhat move the belly downwards'. Toadflax ointment helps ease boils and haemorrhoids and the juice is a good cure for conjunctivitis. When boiled in milk it makes an excellent fly poison. A few plants laid in chickens' drinking water act as a reviver for them in hot weather.

Great Mullein *Verbascum thapsus* is a tall
handsome plant of drier places and looks very
impressive in a herb garden. It has been used
to treat bronchial complaints and catarrh in
humans and for cattle for centuries. A tea
made from the flowers helps chest colds and
has a pleasant honey taste. The stalks are very
woolly and were once dipped in suet and
burned as candles.

FIGWORT FAMILY (contd) **Brooklime** *Veronica beccabunga* with its pretty blue flowers grows in marshy places, ditches and ponds all over Europe. It was made into an anti-scorbutic spring drink in the middle ages with Scurvy Grass and Seville Oranges. It is also diuretic and was used as a cure for gout. If it is gathered from clean, fresh water and washed well it can be added to sandwiches and used as a garnish.

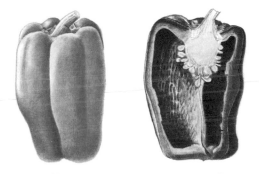

NIGHTSHADE FAMILY **Peppers** *Capsicum anuum* can be easily grown from seed in pots or window boxes on a sunny windowsill or in the greenhouse. Seed should be sown in early spring and kept warm and moist. Seedlings should be potted up singly into pots and the tips pricked out to give a bushy plant. They need plenty of sun and water; overhead spraying will help fruit set. Feed every fortnight as the fruits develop. There are many varieties, red, yellow and green. Paprika, cayenne and chillie are all made from *Capsicium* peppers, and they are delicious as a vegetable or in salads.

197

LIME FAMILY **Common Lime** or **Linden** *Tilia
vulgaris* is very common in Britain and Europe
and is actually a hybrid. A large, handsome
tree, it is often planted in towns and, in early
summer, when it flowers, it fills the air with a
delicious honey-like scent. The flowers can be
used fresh or dried to make a soothing tea
which steadies the nerves and aids the
digestion. Lime tea is also used as a decongest-
ant for chest colds, and it is supposed to
prevent clogging of the veins by excess
cholesterol. An extract of lime bark was once
used as a cure for herpes. Lime flowers make
a relaxing bath. The wood is used for fine
carvings and musical instruments. Young lime
leaves can be added fresh to sandwiches and
salads. Honey bees love lime flowers which, as
anyone who has parked their car under a lime
tree will know, produce copious nectar. Lime
honey is quite delicious. If you are about to
plant a lime tree do not plant *T. tomentosa* cv.
'petiolaris', which is poisonous to bees.

Nasturtium Family **Nasturtium** *Tropaeolum majus* is a very attractive trailing plant with bright orange or yellow flowers. It is an annual which grows well up fences and will soon spread over odd corners, compost heaps and over tree stumps. It will grow well almost anywhere, given a light soil and a sunny position. The dwarf variety is more suitable for confined spaces and flower borders. Planted between vegetables, Nasturtium will attract insect pests away from them, they are very susceptible to Blackfly. Leaves can be cut before flowering for use in salads and sandwiches and chopped into cottage cheese,

they have a fresh peppery tang and should be used sparingly at first. The leaves were once thought to purge the brain and enliven people, they are rich in vitamin C and can be used as an antibiotic. The flowers look very pretty in salads. The ribbed seeds can be gathered green and pickled in mild vinegar, they taste like peppery capers.

Umbellifer Family **Dill** *Anethum graveolens* is an annual, easily grown from seed and suitable for window boxes. The plant is short-lived, if planted at intervals up to midsummer it should provide a constant supply of fresh leaves. It is a hardy annual and can be sown in a sunny, sheltered place in early spring to provide seeds later on. Seedlings should be thinned out, they do not transplant well. Once established, dill should re-sow itself in the same spot for years. Plant a few seeds in April or May to have fresh seeds in time for your cucumber pickling. Different varieties are grown for seeds or leaves. Dill is rather susceptible to aphids. Leaves should be gathered for drying before flowering. For pickling cut the tops with both leaves and seedheads attached. Dill has a sharp aromatic, slightly aniseed flavour, and the leaves can be added to vegetables, salads, fish and fruit dishes. It is carminative, helps the digestion, and is used in gripe water. The seeds can be chewed to freshen the breath and are mildly soporific to babies. A tisane of dill seeds is good for hiccoughs and vomiting, and with aniseed, chamomile and hop shoots is pleasantly soporific.

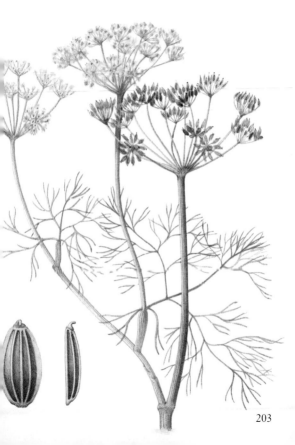

203

1a

UMBELLIFER FAMILY (contd) **Garden Angelica**
Angelica officinalis (**1**) is easily grown from seed and
thrives in gardens everywhere. It grows up to 2m tall
and is very handsome, but really only suitable for
large gardens. It thrives in a good deep moist loam,
with plenty of manure. The plant must be kept
well-watered. If you are collecting stalks for candying
(**1a**) cut off the flower spikes or the plant will die after
flowering. It can sometimes be found as a garden
escape.

True Wild Angelica *A. sylvestris* is a more slender
plant and rather bitter, it is better to use the garden
variety. Its name derives from its angelic powers
against evil spells and witchcraft. The seeds are
carminative and help the digestion. The roots and
stalks help bronchial troubles, coughs and colds.
Angelica is also used to flavour liqueurs, the flavour
is similar to juniper. The leaves can be dried for use
in a tea similar to China tea, for pot pourri and herb
pillows and for a bath herb. An essential oil is
extracted from the fruits and roots for cosmetics,
perfumes and confectionery. When cooked with
rhubarb or gooseberries the roots and stems will, like
Sweet Cecily, remove tartness.

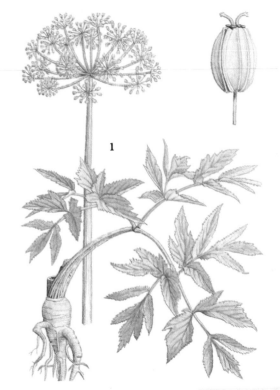

1

UMBELLIFER FAMILY (contd) **Chervil** *Anthriscus cerifolium* was introduced all over Europe by the Romans. It is very easy to grow and leaves can be picked six to eight weeks after the seed is sown. If grown outside it is best to chose the curly-leaved, parsley-like variety, the smooth-leaved variety could be confused with Hemlock – which is extremely poisonous. Sow the seeds in open ground at intervals from March and throughout the summer to ensure a constant supply of fresh leaves during the summer months. For winter use, sow seeds in autumn in pots or windowboxes. The seedlings will not transplant easily. The leaves both freeze and dry well. Flower shoots should be removed to increase the supply of fresh leaves. The plant is likely to bolt if it is allowed to dry out so keep it well-watered, in a damp soil, in semi-shade. Chervil juice was once used for cases of jaundice and gout, it also reduces fevers and promotes sweating. An infusion of the leaves also aids digestion. Chervil soup is famous for its delicate aroma, a true gourmet dish. Chervil is an essential ingredient of *fines herbes* and tends to enhance the flavour of other herbs. It is excellent in omelettes, scrambled eggs and sauces.

207

UMBELLIFER FAMILY (contd) **Caraway** *Carum carvi* is rather rare in the wild in Britain but grows wild in Europe and parts of Asia and is naturalized in some parts of the USA. It is biennial and sown from seed in autumn to flower and seed the following summer. Once established it will re-sow itself. It can be sown in spring and will produce lush greenery which can be used fresh in salads and cream cheese, like parsley. If kept trimmed in the first summer it will flower and seed better the following summer. The seedheads must be cut before spring and hung over a cloth to collect the seeds. The seeds have a sharp spicy taste and can be chewed to freshen the breath, especially after eating garlic, and will relieve indigestion and flatulence. Caraway seed tea relieves chesty colds and can be given to nursing mothers to increase lactation. The seeds are used extensively by the food industry, baked on top of bread and rolls and in cheeses. Add a few seeds to a pan of spring cabbage or to a shredded cabbage salad. The most famous uses for Caraway seeds must be in a really sticky seed cake, and in sweets and liqueur. It was once thought to have powers against evil and witchcraft and was invaluable in love potions.

209

UMBELLIFER FAMILY (contd) **Coriander** *Coriandrum sativum* has, on first encountering it, a rather unpleasant smell, and the leaves have a strong unusual taste, best used in hot curries or as a garnish. The seeds are strongly aromatic, with a warm spicy flavour and a tang of citrus. Seeds can be sown in early spring for the leafy summer growth, or in autumn for seeds the following summer. Plant out in a light, fairly dry, sunny position, seedlings do not transplant well. Leaves can be gathered at any time, they do not dry well. Seedheads should be cut just before ripening and hung over a cloth to collect the seeds. The seeds are, like those of many other umbels, used for their carminative properties, to settle digestive troubles and as a flavouring for nasty medicines. An infusion of the leaves will ease stomach cramps. Coriander ointment soothes stiff joints and rheumatic aches and pains. The seeds are used for flavouring canned fish and are essential in all curries and mixed spice. The leaves ground up with garlic, ginger and mustard seeds are made into chutney. The seed oil is used in perfumery and for flavouring gin. Try Coriander a little at a time at first – it does not agree with everyone.

211

UMBELLIFER FAMILY (contd) **Cumin** *Cuminum cyminum* was once commonly grown in medieval herb gardens for its digestive and anti-flatulent properties and for treating various chest complaints. It was also widely used to disguise the taste of 'off' meat. It is an annual, seeds should be sown in early spring, under glass or on a sunny windowsill, and planted out into a sunny, well-drained position in a rich soil when danger of frost is past. The small pink or white flowers precede seeds similar to Caraway which drop easily. Seedheads should be cut just before ripening and hung upside-down where seed can drop on to a paper. The seed can be chewed whole to calm minor digestive troubles and flatulence. An infusion of ground seeds has a warming effect on the whole body and will soothe coughs, colds and 'flu symptoms. The seeds are delicious roasted in a dry pan and sprinkled on bread and buns or added to yoghurt relishes for eating with curry. The roasted seeds give a warm spicy flavour to bean stews and also improve digestibility. Cumin seeds are an essential ingredient of Garam Masala and are widely used in Indian cookery. The volatile oils are used in perfumery and liqueurs.

213

UMBELLIFER FAMILY (contd) **Fennel** *Foeniculum vulgare* (**2**) is a must for every herb garden, if you have the room. It also adds height to a herbaceous border and will give off a warm aniseed scent. It is a hardy perennial and can easily be grown from seed in spring and from root divisions in autumn. It will do well almost anywhere in a sunny position. Fennel has been used since the middle ages for eye complaints, to induce sleep and to aid digestion. It was also used in various obscure ceremonies to dispel evil spirits and counter witchcraft. The leaves do not dry well, but the stems can be cut up and dried for winter use. Seeds should be collected as for other umbels. A sprig of leaves inside a baked fish gives it a fresh, sharp, aniseed taste. All parts of the plant in sauces and stuffing help the digestion of fatty meats.

Florence Fennel *F. vulgare azoricum* (**1**) looks like a squat celery and only grows well in northern countries in a very good summer. It can be obtained from most large stores and can be added raw to salad or made into soups. For thousands of years Fennel seeds have been chewed or made into all sorts of recipes to cure obesity.

214

215

Umbellifer Family (contd) **Lovage** *Levisticum officinalis* may be too large for the average herb garden. It is perennial, after a few years it develops a sturdy rootstock and may grow up to 3.5m (10ft) tall in a good year. If you do have room, it is a very impressive and useful plant. It can be grown from seed or by root division and likes a deep, damp, well-drained soil. Seed should be sown as soon as it is ripe. Roots can be divided up in autumn or early spring. Two plants should be enough for most purposes, one kept trimmed for fresh leafy growth and the other allowed to flower. Leaves dry well and seedheads should be cut before ripening as with other umbels. The leaves, stalks and seeds all have a strong yeasty smell and flavour, invaluable in vegetarian cookery. The leaves can be used in soups, stews and casseroles or in salads – they add a celery-like flavour. The seeds can be sprinkled on bread and biscuits like fennel and dill. As a bath herb Lovage soothes the joints and stimulates circulation. The leaves make a fragrant tea which can be drunk sweetened or salted and was once taken as an aphrodisiac. An infusion of the leaves is an effective herbal deodorant.

217

UMBELLIFER FAMILY (contd) **Sweet Cecily** *Myrrhis odorata* is a handsome feathery plant in any position. It appears early in the year and the white flowers of early summer give way to very characteristic elongated fruits. It can be grown from fresh seeds in autumn or from root division and likes a moist soil in a semi-shaded position. It will readily seed itself once established. The leaves do not dry well, but fortunately have a long growing season. They have a sweet, aniseed taste and can be eaten in salads or garnishes or cooked with sharp fruits such as gooseberries, plums and rhubarb so that less sugar is needed. Excellent for slimmers. The seeds can be dried and used all the year round. They have similar properties to the leaves but a much stronger flavour and can be used in most dishes instead of cloves. The roots can be grated into salads or cooked like choice parsnips. Culpepper made Sweet Cecily into a compress for bruises and swellings. An infusion of the leaves or crushed seeds was once used for warming the stomach and stimulating the appetite. The seeds are mildly laxative. The roots were once made into concoctions to give protection against plague.

218

219

UMBELLIFER FAMILY (contd) **Wild Parsnip** *Pastinaca sativa* is the ancestor of cultivated parsnip and can be found on wasteland in grassy and bare places, especially on limey soils. It has umbels of yellow flowers, and stems and leaves which smell strongly when bruised. the thin, tough roots can be used as a vegetable but are sweeter than cultivated parsnips and better suited to grating into biscuits and buns. An infusion of the roots is diuretic, soothing and stimulates the appetite.

Burnet Saxifrage *Pimpinella saxifraga* is a perennial herb of dry chalk and limestone meadows, verges and wastelands. The young lower leaves look similar to Salad Burnet and can be used in salads and sauces. Drugs are extracted from the roots for use as diuretics, to stimulate the digestion and to ease respiratory troubles. An infuson of the leaves can be taken for catarrh or flatulence, or it can be used as a gargle. In medieval times it was believed to ward off plague.

UMBELLIFER FAMILY **Parsley** *Petroselinum crispum* (**1**) must be our most familiar and universal herb, probably originating in the eastern Mediterranean. It is very easy to grow, even in a small pot on the kitchen windowsill, and can be used to flavour a wide variety of dishes. It is biennial but is usually only grown for the first year's leaves, in its second year the plants go straggly and flower. The seeds can take several weeks to germinate and should be prevented from drying out. The leaves can be used fresh in sauces, salads, mayonnaise, soups and for garnishing; they dry or freeze well. Parsley in a white sauce is excellent with fish, parsley butter or yoghurt is very good in baked potatoes. Leaves are best dried in a hot oven and stored in airtight jars. There are many varieties, such as Curly and Fern-leaved Parsley. Parsley leaves are rich in vitamins A, B and C and iron. Parsley tea, made from dried leaves, is a mild diuretic and will soothe rheumatic pains. Parsley water was once used to remove freckles. Parsley is also used to flavour dog food. The seeds are poisonous if taken in quantity.

Hamburg Parsley *P. crispum* 'Tuberosum' (**2**) is grown for its carroty roots, gathered in autumn, which can be eaten like parsnips or grated into salads. The dried roots can be used for flavouring.

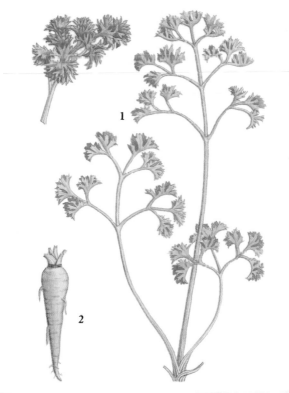

1

2

223

UMBELLIFER FAMILY (contd) **Alexanders** or **Black Lovage** *Smyrnium olusatrum* was introduced into Northern Europe by the Romans and now grows wild, especially near the sea. It can be grown from seeds sown in late summer. It is eaten as a vegetable, the young shoots are boiled and lose their aniseed smell on cooking; the boiled flower buds are very good with capers. It was once commonly eaten with fish dishes on days of 'fasting and abstinence' and was grown in monastery gardens for treating various ailments, including snakebite and colic, and to aid the expulsion of afterbirth.

Aniseed *Pimpinella anisum* is a native of the Middle East and does not always seed properly in temperate climates. Sow seeds in light soil and a sunny position in late spring. The leaves have a more delicate flavour than the seeds and can be used fresh in salads and with vegetables, soft cheese and yoghurt dishes. The seeds are widely used for flavouring sweets, cakes, liqueurs and toothpaste, in mouse poison and in pot pourri. Chew a few seeds to freshen the breath, aid the digestion, soothe headaches and relieve catarrh.

VALERIAN FAMILY **Lamb's Lettuce** or **Corn Salad**
Valerianella locusta is no longer the common cornfield
weed that it once was in Britain but it is still common
in Europe. It can sometimes be found in waste places
and on old walls in the south of England. it grows into
a short spindly plant with clusters of tiny lilac flowers,
not at all like Valerian. It can be sown in seed trays
in the greenhouse in late summer to provide tender
salads throughout the winter.

Valerian *Valeriana officinalis* is often seen in damp woods, ditches and marshes all over Europe. It has a rather unpleasant smell when bruised, which may explain its supposed powers over witches and as an aphrodisiac. This smell was very popular in the middle ages for scenting linen and herb baths, it was also used as a spice. Valerian is famous for its use as a sedative and pain killer and for treating nervous disorders. Valerian oil was once used for flavouring white wine. It was also associated with the Virgin Mary.

227

VIOLET FAMILY **Sweet Violet** *Viola odorata* (**1**) has many romantic associations, mostly of Victorian origin. It grows in hedgebanks in Britain and northern Europe and is naturalized in parts of the USA. There are white and violet varieties. The flowers can be eaten fresh in salads, dried for pot pourri or crystallized into sweets for cake decorations. The flowers have a fresh, delicate perfumey flavour and go well in milk puddings, cream and ice cream. Violet syrup is good for chest and throat infections

2

and is a mild laxative. An infusion of the flowers mixed with honey was used to soothe headaches, insomnia and nervousness. Culpepper made cold compresses of violets to apply to 'grieved places', once used extensively for ear infections.

Heartsease *V. tricolor* (**2**) is still common on banks and cultivated fields throughout Europe. A drug extracted from the flowers is made into cough remedies and acne preparations. It was also used to treat venereal diseases.

Glossary of Plant, Culinary and Medical Terms

Anaesthetic causes loss of sensation
Analgesic pain relieving
Anthelmintic kills worms
Antibiotic inhibits growth of germs
Anticoagulant prevents blood clotting
Antidote counteracts poison
Antispasmodic prevents muscular spasms
Arteriosclerosis hardening of the arteries
Astringent causing contractions of skin pores and checking secretions

Carminative relieving windiness (flatulence)
Catarrh inflammation of mucous lining of nose
Colic acute abdominal pain
Compress a dressing applied tightly
Cultivar or **cv.** plant with characteristics selected in cultivation

Decoction water extract of herbs
Demulcent relieves irritation
Deodorant helps prevent body odour
Depressant sedative
Dermatitis inflammation of the skin
Diuretic increasing flow of urine
Dyspesia impaired digestion of food

Escape plant now growing wild, originally introduced from abroad for gardens

Emetic causes vomiting

Essential oil volatile oil prepared from a herb

Expectorant promotes coughing to clear congestion

Flatulence gas in the gut

Febrifuge reduces fever

Fixative oily substance, improves keeping qualities of perfumes

Haemorrhage loss of blood from wound or lesion, external or internal

Haemorrhoids varicose veins of the rectum

Haemostatic staunches bleeding

Hepatitis inflammation of the liver

Hypertension abnormally low blood pressure

Infusion extract made like a tea by pouring boiling water over herbs and allowing to stand

Lactation formation and secretion of milk

Laxative loosens bowels

Liniment oily preparation for rubbing on affected parts

Mucilage gelatinous (jelly-like) substance

Narcotic having numbing, stupefying or sleep-inducing effect

Native occuring naturally in that area

Purgative very powerful laxative

Poultice dressing, usually hot, applied to reduce inflammation

Runners stems growing along ground, producing roots

Sedative calming or sleep inducing

Stigma female   part of flower which receives pollen

Stimulant increasing activity

Stomachic beneficial to digestion

Styptic staunches bleeding

Tincture medicinal extract prepared by solution in alcohol

Toxic poisonous

Variety or **var.** naturally occuring plant, differing slightly from main species

Vermifuge destroys and expels intestinal worms

Volatile oil fragrant plant oil

Vulnerary heals wounds

Index of Common Names

Index of Scientific Names

2

LABIAE FAMILY **Hyssop** *Hyssopus officinalis* grows wild in dry stony places in the Mediterranean region. It is not difficult to cultivate in a sunny well-drained position with light, sandy soil and can be grown from seeds or cuttings. It makes a bushy, very aromatic plant, usually blue-flowered, but there are white and pink forms. The leaves should be cut before flowering if they are to be dried. It is used in cough remedies and gargles to alleviate hoarseness. The leaves and flowering shoots can make an infusion which is a stimulant and expectorant, and also aids the digestion. Hyssop is used as a flavouring in liqueurs, particularly Absinthe and Chartreuse. It has a minty, slightly bitter taste and is good as a garnish, rendering fatty meats such as duck or sausages more digestible. Try it with stewed apricots. It is an excellent herb for attracting bees and butterflies to the garden and should be mixed into pot pourri. It was once used for strewing and nosegays.

107

Labiate Family (contd) **Ground Ivy** *Glechoma hederacea* is a very familiar, short, creeping plant of woods and hedgerows throughout Europe and the British Isles. The whole plant is strongly aromatic and it is found in snuff and herbal tobacco. It was used to flavour ale before hops were introduced into England, hence its other name of 'ale-hoof'. An infusion of the leaves makes a soothing eyewash or, mixed with honey and liquorice, a tasty cough cure. It was once a favourite remedy for lunacy.

White Deadnettle *Lamium album*, despite its name and nettle-like leaves, is unrelated to the nettles. The white flowers produce abundant nectar, are popular with insects and very sweet to chew. The young leaves can be used as a vegetable and in quiches or omelettes. They have been used medicinally for a variety of purposes from easing aching joints and nosebleeds to treating infected hangnails and gout. An effective herbal shampoo can be made by boiling soapwort with white deadnettle leaves – it is very mild and good for greasy hair.

LABIATE FAMILY (contd) **English Lavender** *Lavandula augustifolia*, originally a Mediterranean plant, is an evergreen shrub, once very common in cottage gardens, which makes a pretty border to paths and flowerbeds. There are many other types of lavender, such as *L. stoechas*, which is very pretty, but not hardy. English Lavender is best for most purposes. It should be grown in an open, sunny position. In the northern hemisphere cuttings with a heel can be taken in August and kept in a cold frame, or planted outside in a sheltered place in October. Well-grown plants can be divided in spring. Bushes should be kept trimmed. A drug made from Lavender is a digestive aid, cures flatulence and is an antiseptic. The leaves can be used in cooking like Rosemary, but have a harsher flavour. A few spikes of Lavender put in a jar with sugar gives it a pleasant flowery taste. Lavender flowers are an essential ingredient for pot pourri, lavender bags, toilet water, perfumes and as a bath herb. 'Dwarf Munstead' and 'Hidcote' are good varieties.

111

LABIATE FAMILY **Lemon Verbena** *Lippia citriodora* is a must for every herb enthusiast. It grows as a small bush, with bright green pointed leaves in whorls, but having originated in South America is not hardy. It can easily be grown in a pot and kept in a cool frost-free place in winter but put outdoors in the summer. It is a good houseplant, for although the flowers are unspectacular it gives off a delicate lemony scent when brushed against. It needs a poor soil, must never be over-watered and can be propagated from cuttings. The leaves must be harvested for drying before the plant flowers and can be used like lavender to scent linen and in pot pourri. A delicate tisane made from the leaves is popular in continental Europe and the leaves can be used to flavour fruit drinks, jams and jellies and make an interesting alternative to lemon in a cup of tea. It is also very good with fish.

LABIATE FAMILY **White Horehound** *Marrubium vulgare* can often be found in dry pastures and waste places. The flowering shoots were made into a drug for bronchial complaints and cough medicines and used as a digestive aid for consumptives. The plant is slightly bitter and is put in Passover dishes. It was once used as a shoe-lining – not to prevent foot odour but to stop dogs snapping at the heels. Horehound candy is made by boiling the leaves in sugar and hanging them by the stalks to dry.

Bergamot *Monarda didyma* is a tall handsome perennial producing spikes of whorled flowers in red, pink, purple, white or lavender It is propagated from root divisions and should be split up annually. It originates in America and the leaves and flowers make the soporific 'Oswego tea', much used by the Indians and taken up by patriotic Americans at the time of the Boston Tea Party. The red-flowered form is best for tea, giving it an interesting colour. Bergamot can also be used to flavour wine, fruit drinks and real tea.

LABIATE FAMILY (contd) **Lemon Balm** *Melissa officinalis* is a vigorous, leafy plant from southern Europe, very common in gardens and often found as an escape in shady spots. It can be propagated from seeds, cuttings or root division in spring and is very easy to grow. There is an attractive variety with variegated leaves. Leaves should be collected for drying before flowering. An infusion of the leaves can be used for nervous stomach cramps, vomiting and insomnia. It is very soothing and can help relaxation and dispel incipient migraine. The leaves are also very tasty in China tea and cold drinks and are popular in continental Europe in salads and omelettes. It can be used instead of lemon peel in soups, stews and fruit dishes and in Switzerland is a flavouring for cheese. It makes a soothing bath herb for aching joints and the dried leaves can be put into pot pourri.

LABIATE FAMILY (contd) **The Mints** *Mentha* spp.
There are many different species and varieties of
mints, with quite different flavours. They tend to
grow vigorously and to spread by runners so it is
advisable to separate different mints by barriers of
sunken slates, or by planting them in pots. They like
a warm, moist, sheltered position, well-manured.
Frequent cutting improves their bushiness but do not
allow them to flower. All are very easily grown from
runners planted out into a rich, moist soil in spring,
after the last frosts, or into a sheltered position in
early autumn. The leaves taste best if grown in
semi-shade.
Spearmint *Mentha spicata* (**1**) is most often found in

gardens, it has a very familiar flavour and the oil is used in toothpaste and chewing gum.

Apple Mint *M. rotundifolia* (**2**) has a more appley flavour and is very good in cold drinks.

Water Mint *M. aquatica* (**3**) is similar in properties to Peppermint (p. 120) and has the strongest medicinal effect, especially for stomach upsets.

Pineapple Mint *M. rotundifolia variegata* (**4**) is shorter than the others and has attractive variegated leaves and a fruity flavour. It grows very lush if picked often.

Ginger Mint *M. x gentilis* 'Variegata' (**5**) is also well worth growing for flavouring cold drinks and puddings.

1

2

LABIATE FAMILY Mints (contd) **Bowles Mint** *Mentha rotundifolia* Bowles var. (**1**) has rather fleshy, woody leaves and grows over 1m (3ft) tall. It is best for mint sauce.

Peppermint *M. piperita* (**2**) makes the best mint tea. The leaves dry easily and can be crunched up and stored in airtight jars.

Eau de Cologne Mint *M. citrata* (**3**) has a lemony flavour and can be used in cold drinks and pot pourri.

Pennyroyal *M. pulegium* (**4**) makes a refreshing tea which should ease depression – a sprig in a jug of drinking water is very refreshing.